T0077883

BECOMING AN ORDERS EXPERT
A GUIDE ON SEEKING AND MAKING SPIRITUAL ORDERS

MARTHA LYNETTE ALEXANDER & NATASHA A. CUMBERBATCH RYAN

WESTBOW
PRESS®
A DIVISION OF THOMAS NELSON
& ZONDERVAN

Copyright © 2017 Martha Lynette Alexander & Natasha A. Cumberbatch Ryan.

All rights reserved. No part of this book may be used or reproduced by any means, graphic, electronic, or mechanical, including photocopying, recording, taping or by any information storage retrieval system without the written permission of the author except in the case of brief quotations embodied in critical articles and reviews.

This book is a work of non-fiction. Unless otherwise noted, the author and the publisher make no explicit guarantees as to the accuracy of the information contained in this book and in some cases, names of people and places have been altered to protect their privacy.

WestBow Press books may be ordered through booksellers or by contacting:

WestBow Press
A Division of Thomas Nelson & Zondervan
1663 Liberty Drive
Bloomington, IN 47403
www.westbowpress.com
1 (866) 928-1240

Because of the dynamic nature of the Internet, any web addresses or links contained in this book may have changed since publication and may no longer be valid. The views expressed in this work are solely those of the author and do not necessarily reflect the views of the publisher, and the publisher hereby disclaims any responsibility for them.

Any people depicted in stock imagery provided by Thinkstock are models, and such images are being used for illustrative purposes only.
Certain stock imagery © Thinkstock.

Scripture quotations taken from the Amplified® Bible (AMP), Copyright © 2015 by The Lockman Foundation. Used by permission. www.Lockman.org

Scripture quotes marked (KJV) are taken from the King James Version of the Bible.

Scripture quotations marked (ESV) are from the ESV® Bible (The Holy Bible, English Standard Version®), copyright © 2001 by Crossway, a publishing ministry of Good News Publishers. Used by permission. All rights reserved.

Scripture quotations marked (NIV) are taken from the Holy Bible, New International Version®, NIV®. Copyright © 1973, 1978, 1984, 2011 by Biblica, Inc.™ Used by permission of Zondervan. All rights reserved worldwide.

ISBN: 978-1-9736-0906-3 (sc)
ISBN: 978-1-9736-0907-0 (hc)
ISBN: 978-1-9736-0905-6 (e)

Library of Congress Control Number: 2017916747

Print information available on the last page.

WestBow Press rev. date: 11/17/2017

To Vernon Cumberbatch (deceased) and Angela Birche, my father and mother, who taught me to reverence and respect God; Martin Ryan, my darling husband, who challenges me every day to be a better me, much love and many thanks; Alexander Dumas Matthews (deceased), Anna Matthews-Peeples and Inez McIntosh, my family and pillars of support, many thanks; and Tristan Micah Alexander, my gift from God. Tristan, you continue to endure, without complaint, a mother who writes more than she speaks; I love you endlessly and thank God daily for blessing me with a son like you.

Our lives find meaning because you were all part of our purposes.

Acknowledgement

The lifespan for writing this book was short, as willed by God, and the many people He sent into our paths to aid with the process must be acknowledged and lauded for their contribution in helping us bring this work to completion. First, we must thank God the Father for trusting us with the revelation that He is order and for using us as channels for this truth. And to the Holy Spirit, who actually wrote this truth through us, thanks for using us as pens and erasers to write down this truth; and for revisiting and refining our every word and weeding out anything of self that God did not want included. To You, our dear Holy Spirit, we give a resounding hallelujah that it is finished. You are indeed the inspiration and best Editor any author would have been privileged to work with, and we could not have done this without You. Then to Jesus Christ, our Saviour and Lord and soon coming King, we say cheers; for Your life has inspired us to walk in humility after You and to give our lives to God to be used as He wills.

Without You, precious Jesus, we would not have been able to present ourselves as willing writing instruments for this work, so may it serve to glorify Your name and bring order to Your church, paving the path for Your imminent return.

This work was helped by many whom our God placed in our paths, and so we clap our hands in appreciation and thanksgiving for their contribution. To Rayna Braxton of Pennsylvania, USA, for reading and giving us feedback as we wrote, we say thanks. Your excitement and encouragement as you read disjointed pieces of this manuscript and your simple questions seeking clarification helped us to revisit and simplify so that all readers would understand the content. So thumbs up for your selfless contribution. To Candice Cielto Jones of Maraval, Trinidad and Tobago, for so willingly providing feedback on this manuscript and for asking those rather insightful and discerning questions, which caused us to reread and massage this work into what it is, we say that you were sent, for this time, to play this role. Wholehearted thanks Candice; you are a gem, and our desire is that you will find nuggets of truth in this book that will answer some of the questions you have and bring an end to your searching. We pray order for you and declare that even as you make yourself available to be found by Christ Jesus, He will reveal more of Himself to you. To Nekeisha Bishop of Port of Spain, Trinidad and Tobago, we say thanks, sweetheart.

You alone know the contribution you have made and its immense value to this work, and for this we are forever indebted. The God who is order did not join you to us by chance, and His designs for your life will unfold in due course. To Thomas Mussio of Trinidad and Tobago for coming at the right point and providing your creative expertise in designing that impressive cover for our book, you have our eternal gratitude. You were the instrument used by the Holy Spirit to bring to completion this assignment. Thomas, thank you for your obedience to the leading of the Holy Spirit and for allowing Him to use you in this profound way. And finally, to our family members, you have been tireless and uncomplaining in your support; may order manifest to you and in you, in the same way it has to us, and may the God who is order envelop you in His mercy and reward your faithfulness a hundredfold.

CONTENTS

CHAPTER 7: WHY BE AN ORDERS EXPERT? . . 186

PREFACE

This book goes far behind the curtain, into an area that no biblical scholar has touched in any in-depth and direct way before now. It presents God as order and makes the case in a simple and straightforward way as to why He requires His church to walk in this 'new' yet old revelation of who He is. God has always been order and was first presented as such at the beginning of creation, and He continued to manifest as order throughout biblical history and even into this present time. While miniscule, if any, doctrinal attention has been given to this aspect of God's nature and character, it is an incontestable fact that God is order. Why He is calling focus to this aspect of His nature now and directing His children to become orders experts has to do with His end-time plan for His church.

God began speaking to me about writing when I was a teenager, and I did; but it was only recently that He made it clear that I was required to write many books, including spiritual works. I knew there were books in me to be written, and wherever I went, I was being told that in confirmation. I was unsettled in my spirit and questioning God about what He required me to write on next, and not hearing from Him clearly but hearing only that I was to write. I remember that while walking down the corridor in my home one day, conversing with God, I turned to Him and asked, 'Well, what do You want me to write? I can't just write if I have nothing to write about.' I felt then that I heard Him say 'order', but as I am wont to do at times when I am in uncertain and unfamiliar territory, I proceeded to ignore what I had heard. In my mind, God really could not be seriously telling me to write about order; it was so far-fetched and incomprehensible to me. What did He want me to write about order? I felt that I knew nothing about order, so what would I write about? So I placed that conversation behind me and kept pressing forward with life and with writing nothing. On several occasions thereafter, I kept hearing the word 'order' and dismissing it as mind over matter. Then my spiritual daughter, Natasha, visited, and in conversations, we discussed the concept of order. But still walking in dismissive stubbornness, I sat on the direct command of my Father to me to write about 'order', justifying my non-action with the excuse that I did not know anything about order so could not write about it. I felt that, of course, God would understand and respect my position. Then, on 16 March 2017, while sitting in the most unlikely of places during a quiet few minutes, I drew my computer to me and began writing. As the words tumbled out, unhindered and seamlessly, I knew this book was not about me or about what limited knowledge I possessed on order; it was about God and allowing myself to be used as His writing instrument through His Holy Spirit. It was about God as order and me as His writing pen, through which He would present order.

Since I began writing this book, my life has changed dramatically; situations I was dealing with began unravelling in different ways; my approaches and perspectives on many issues in my life began to morph into unique insights for solutions, and strangely, I gained peace in many unsettled situations and a new weapon of laughter to deal with issues that were previously clouding my life. How funny it is to be used as someone's pen and to have your life rewritten, refocused and rejuvenated almost in front your face as you write. This work is of God and to His name only belongs the glory. I am required by God only to walk in obedience by beginning my journey of becoming an orders expert. I have started. The reach of this work is in His hands. God indeed is order!

Martha Lynette Alexander

Becoming an orders expert started for me, Natasha, as I sat in the back of an auditorium, listening to my mentor and spiritual mother speaking to her first-year law school students about how to write orders. She had walked onto that compound that March 2017 afternoon and begun to teach on the topic of legal orders. I am always intrigued by her passion and ability to impart knowledge to her students – especially to me. She is gifted and anointed to teach in whatever arena God sends her. After the two-hour teaching session, during which I had lapped up every word uttered by her, I wanted to impress her with my recall skills. As we were driving home, I began regurgitating the content of her lesson, and for the remainder of that day, we were deliberating and discussing orders in various contexts. I remember telling her that mankind was so disorderly and that there seemed to be an unleashing of disorder and confusion in the body of Christ and in the world. She agreed profusely and then suggested that maybe she should write a book on orders. The rest is history.

So when the divine call came for me to be a co-author of this book, it was exhilarating yet challenging. I knew that God had purposed me for this season, for this time, and as the writing progressed, the revelation of this level of spiritual warfare began to have a greater impact on my prayer life. In my own life, there were numerous situations that were plaguing me and preventing the glory of God from being shown in my circumstances. There was one particular test that was the hardest I ever had to face, and it pained me to my very core, although I had accepted God's word concerning it. I was convinced God would give me the victory. I believed it. I claimed it. I had faith in God that it would happen.

So when we started this book on becoming an orders expert, I began to gain clarity on all the chaos and confusion in my own life, and as I heeded the call to embrace and receive the truth that God *is* order rather than just a God of order, I felt my whole life was being turned topsy-turvy and the door of change was opening. First, I, who was literally the epitome of an unskilled praying Christian, was beginning to turn into a skilled, strategic, and confident prayer warrior, through acquiring a better understanding of spiritual orders. I knew this transformation was possible only because I had embraced the simple profound truth that God is order. Secondly, I began praying for God to change my perspective on my situation. As we wrote about the various orders, I simultaneously began utilising them, knowing that I desired a life-altering experience from God and that I was about to receive it. I placed my application for an appeal before God and waited, for now I was viewing scriptures I had appropriated to my situation differently, including, 'Ask and it will be given to you; seek and you will find; knock and the door will be opened to you' (Matthew 7:7 NIV). We were given a timeframe of three months to complete this work, and I saw God literally push us to a near stage of completion within a five-week period; I waited for the time to be abridged for delivery of my miracle.

Natasha Cumberbatch Ryan

INTRODUCTION

RIVETING, GROUND-BREAKING, AND COMPELLING

This book challenges all believers in Christ to acknowledge what they have always known deep within – that God is order. It presents the ground-breaking truth that God is, has always been, and will forever be the God who is order. It makes a clarion call to every Christian, no matter where he or she is in his or her walk with Christ, to desire more and to reach for and exercise the power encapsulated in this revelation that God is order. This book is a must read for every Christian who desires to fine-tune his or her praying skills and to ascend to a higher level of strategic spiritual warfare. It brings a new and advanced understanding of what is meant by 'praying strategically', by clarifying prior misconceptions and setting in order many erroneous practices existing in the church. It is simply an eye-opening presentation of God as order, and it charts the course for using this revelation to launch an attack or counterattack against the plans of Satan.

No one will read this book and be unchanged by the unique, fresh, and compelling presentation of spiritual orders and the God who is order. It calls on the believer to look at self, have a truthful discourse on the flaws in self and in the church, and seek to right them now, in the face of Jesus' imminent return. It will capsize erroneous practices, lift covers on the hold of sin in the church, bring healing through honest introspection, and equip believers with new spiritual warfare approaches to wipe out the enemy.

Becoming an Orders Expert is inspired by the Holy Spirit and written for this present time, to bring believers into the fullness of the understanding, knowledge, and demonstration of Jesus Christ.

Chapter 1

The Power of Order

God is order. This is by far the single most powerful statement of truth about God, yet it continues to defy the understanding of humanity. This simple statement is so powerful that it will revolutionise your life if you come to a full understanding of what it means. I recall when the Holy Spirit first impressed upon me that the God whom I serve is not just a God of order but actually *is* order. At that time, I was already familiar with the power contained in an order made by the court system in which I worked, and I knew how orders affected the lives of litigants who frequented the judicial system on a daily basis. I understood better than most the powerful impact of orders issued by the court to change lives, to remedy problems, to quell disturbances, to stop problems from continuing, and to bring relief to many a situation. I understood then that a court order was influential and represented more than just victory in a battle; it was the key to unlocking previously closed doors, and it fixed many intractable problems. I understood that in some situations, if a person did not have an order, his or her circumstances would never change. I understood that an order is a tool of empowerment; it can cause walls to crumble, and it can immediately put a halt to attacks in the physical realm.

An order is an instrument with a wide reach that can bring healing and ward off or destroy attacks from one's enemies. An order has the power to bring about the demise of a person or a situation. Its power was accepted and respected by me. I knew that a person dare not question a validly issued order of the court, and if that did indeed happen, there would be serious consequences to be faced. I also knew that an order could be challenged successfully in the court system, once there were valid grounds for so doing, but that it would only be superseded by another court order. Once an order is signed, sealed, and issued by the court, it stands (unless and until it is appealed, reversed, amended, superseded, set aside, or replaced with another order). An order is used in this earthly system to solve problems – legal, social, political, financial, emotional, domestic, environmental, business, medical, and even regional, and international problems. This meant, to me, that a court order was ultimately 'the fixer'.

I was, therefore, a bit taken aback when the Holy Spirit began speaking to me about order – but not as I understood it to be in the physical, earthly court system. Instead the Holy Spirit spoke to me about order in the church, about divine order, about making spiritual orders, and about God as order. My relationship with God at that time was unique and can best be described as an Edenic relationship. Okay, that term may be confusing to some, so let me explain. Some people have a formal relationship with God, but I didn't, and I never desired that. To me God was my spiritual daddy, and my relationship with Him was informal, communal, and close. In fact, I have always been one to relate to God and have Him relate to me, as I felt He did with Adam in the garden of Eden. This meant that I stood in awe and naked before Him, bare and blameless by the blood of His Son, Jesus Christ. But I also stood knowing that I was unworthy yet counted worthy to converse openly with Him. My prayer life was a conversation with my Father, and there was nothing excluded; I could speak to Him about anything, and likewise, He could speak to me about anything. I needed not nice-sounding words or even words to pray. I was tapped into Him, and He into me; so as I walked, I talked. So when He told me to write about order, I was quick to ask Him, *Why me?* I felt unworthy to be used as a vessel to communicate His message to His people, and I thought that there were others more learned, more skilled, and better equipped to teach on this topic. It was then that He said to me that my life's experiences were not by chance or for my benefit or professional progress, but for His use in His kingdom. He had gifted me with the skill of a teacher and a writer's pen for His use. He had placed me in the earthly court system, in the department I stayed in for seven years, so that I would become an orders expert in the earthly and heavenly courts. He then promoted me to a seat where I was required to pronounce orders that affected people's lives on a daily basis. By then I had been schooled in crafting orders as documents, and now I was engaged in the granting of these orders with the full force of the law behind me. By that time, I had developed a sensitivity, a respect, and a knowing about the nature, impact, and reach of an order in the earthly realm – and it was now time to apply that learning to the divine realm.

I knew I was not required to write about spiritual orders only, but I was told to write about order as a divine principle and how it is applied to my Christian walk; I was also told to write about order in the church and about God as order. It was a mammoth task, I felt, for I had never heard of any doctrine of order. I had attended Bible school and was taught the doctrines of God and the doctrines of humans, but I was not taught about order in this way. I was never schooled in the concept of order and had never given that lacuna in my Christian indoctrination a second thought. It was not that I thought it was unimportant; I had just never even thought about it. But during one of my daily walks with God, He directed me to look around for the materials and began increasing my perception and level of discernment. In the process, I was able to fire up my analytical and comparative skills. I was working in an environment in which the concept of order, as a standard that is set to be adhered to and respected, was stiffly implemented. I was surrounded daily by a strict and formalised structure, where rules and order were mainstays. It was then that I understood why my training had taken the turns it had and that it had been done by divine design and for divine purpose – and that all was meant to influence the kingdom of God.

One of the first things spoken to me by the Holy Spirit was that I was to explain why God is more than just a God of order and why it is significant for the church to grasp this understanding and move quickly into it. Walking in the revelation that God is order – and not simply a God of order – was to move to the next level of my spiritual Edenic walk with God. There was an urgent need for this concept to be grasped, digested, and operationalized, since its converse – disorder, along with its familial cohorts chaos and confusion – was the end-time spirit unleashed upon the world to pave the way for the father of disorder to re-emerge. I knew from the way the Holy Spirit was pressing me that the distinction was important and that I was not merely to gloss over it; I needed to seek to impress upon His people that order is who He is. I knew there would be some who would quickly say they understood although they did not, or some who would try to brush off this new revelation as inconsequential or minimise its import. There would even be those who would seek to discredit it. But I knew that what I was hearing from God was foundational truth that He was now revealing – from a different perspective, precept upon precept, line upon line, here a little and there a little. (See Isaiah 28:13 KJV.) I knew also why He needed me to be the channel for this truth, since my life's experiences had created within me a steely, fearless, and independent nature that stubbornly listened only to what I felt the voice of God was saying. God's Word was my standard, and everything was weighed and assessed against that order.

The very first question I had to confront was why it was easier for individuals to accept that God is a God of order than it was for them to understand that God *is* order. The answer came quickly and with clarity: seeing Him as a God of order is a softer concept, since it suggests that this is a quality He likes and wants to have manifested. This viewpoint gives each individual a bligh.[1] It renders order in and around the person aspirational but not mandatory in a Christian's walk. It externalises the concept, and falsely so, rather than presenting it as an integral part of who God is. Whoopee! Jeez! Yikes! I found myself hopping and jumping around and wanting to scream at the world that no, no, no – order is more than an aspirational quality for God and is more than just a desired behavioural pattern. Order is God, and God is order! Without God there is no order, and without order there is no God. Bam! There it is – the *rhema* word; God and order are intricately interwoven and inseparable concepts. Just as much as we can accept that God is love or that God is our light and salvation, we must accept that God is order.

Almost instantaneously on this revelation becoming crystal clear to me, I felt a burning within me that if humanity were to fail to understand that God is order, we could perish. I had to write; I had to use my pen to make the whole world see and understand what I was seeing. It had become so clear to me that I knew I wanted others to get it as clearly, so I needed to pen all the thoughts flooding through my brain and spirit. I began to understand order versus disorder, God as order, and God acting upon disorder and the role played by God in both. In the first instance, it is His nature or who He is, and in the case of disorder, it is how He acts. I felt the Holy Spirit impress upon me that God operates upon disorder to bring order – as He did in the beginning of the biblical world, and as He now does in present time – to heal, restore, regenerate, and recreate; but He is not disorder and never can be. God operating in times of disorder was also seen in the times of Noah and throughout biblical history, but God was never a part of disorder or a God of disorder. (See Genesis 6; 7 KJV.) Wherever you see disorder, God is operating as the fixer; He is not disorder. There is order in disorder but never disorder in order, for order is a singular and immutable concept; it is unchanging, unchallengeable, and absolute because God is order.

By this time, this new wine was flooding and overflowing from me and I was beside myself as the Holy Spirit continued to pour more of this understanding into me. It was a rhema word that I had received, understanding that without an appreciation of it, I would be partially blind to the end-time events that were unfolding around me globally. I desired deeper and further discernment, so I began crying out to Him for added wisdom. I pressed Him for wisdom, understanding, and knowledge of God as order, and also on how to present this truth. A quick search revealed to me that not much was written about order – and certainly not in the way God was pouring this new wine into me. It was how He wanted it, and He desired that man see that He was always order and presented order.

Order is who God is and always was, but while mankind has moved into deeper and deeper understanding and revelation of God's grace, salvation, love, faith, forgiveness, longsuffering, and other divine principles, he has been slow to appreciate that God is order. Yet this was a foundational divine principle, and I felt impressed by the Holy Spirit that it was an important one – especially for this period. God was calling His people to an understanding of this divine principle now, but it was always a truth that existed from the beginning of time. In submitting and ceding myself to be His writing instrument, the questions came. Wasn't order a primal concept? Didn't God show up as order in the very first chapter of the Bible and throughout? Isn't the world that we inhabit a creation of order? Wasn't everything placed in order by God? Wasn't the Genesis earth then a reflection of order? Wasn't our Genesis God order? So why could man not see that God is order and not just a God of order? I felt then that maybe an understanding of what the word 'order' means will give some insight into the God who is order. It would help place this revelation in its proper spiritual context.

WHAT DOES THE WORD 'ORDER' MEAN?

The Greek words for order, when used as nouns, are 'taxis' and 'tagma'. The former refers to 'an arranging or arrangement', while the latter signifies 'that which has been arranged in order' – 'order' being a military term denoting 'company'. When used as a verb, the words are 'anatassomai', which means 'to arrange in order'; 'diatasso', which means 'to appoint, arrange, charge, give orders to', 'give order', or 'set in order'; or 'epidiorthoo', which means 'to set in order', 'setting right again that which is defective', or 'to restore what has fallen into disorder'.[2] (See Titus 1:5 KJV.) The Hebrew word for order is 'arak', which means 'to arrange or set in order'.[3] It is easy to see how the words and phrases 'an arranging', 'appointing', 'charging', 'giving orders to', 'putting in order', 'setting right again', and 'restoring order' are reflective of God as order. They speak or mirror the essence of who God is when He shows up as order, and what He does. From Genesis to Revelation, God is about order; it is simply who He is, so this is immutable and unchangeable. Because He is order, God presents as order, acts as order, and commands order; which are all Genesis manifestations of who He is.

As order, God is in the business of arranging things in order, which is just one aspect of who He is as order. It is the taxis and tagma sense of God as order. An example of this is seen in the structuring of the fivefold ministries – this is an arranging by God. 'And he gave some, apostles; and some, prophets; and some, evangelists; and some, pastors and teachers; For the perfecting of the saints, for the work of the ministry, for the edifying of the body of Christ' (Ephesians 4:11–12 KJV). This aspect of God arranging ministers in His church into a fivefold grouping is intended to benefit believers by bringing together these gifts and skills to give guidance, governance, protection, training, and grounding to His people. All five gifts are purposed to bring His people into maturity, perfection, and the fullness of the knowledge and demonstration of Christ. 'Till we all come in the unity of the faith, and of the knowledge of the Son of God, unto a perfect man, unto the measure of the stature of the fullness of Christ' (Ephesians 4:13 KJV). Each of the five gifts above has a particular manifestation, and there are some that have a cross-anointing with which they operate; that is to say that ministers may function with more than one anointing or gifting.

In the diatasso sense of God as order, He is involved in appointing order or charging order, which means giving order to things, breathing life into something, or setting things in order. This is the creative order of God, which is also on display in Genesis when He operates as Creator, Life-Giver, and Commander of Order. The concept of charging vividly captures God's innate nature – that of infusing life into, creating, energizing, and producing order. It is the Spirit of God that is moving on the waters in Genesis that is charging, breathing into, arranging, and creating order and, by extension, a world of order.

But God is also epidiorthoo, with this aspect of Him as order referring to His restorative nature; in other words it refers to God as the Restorer-in-Chief of what has fallen into disorder. This is the sense in which He operates in His church, where He is fixing the broken-hearted and unruly behaviour or anything that is defective. The epidiorthoo sense of God is manifested throughout the Old and New Testaments, particularly where His people fall into disorder and He moves to return order. (See Titus 1:5 KJV.) This is also the aspect of God that is presented in His interactions with the murmuring Israelites in the wilderness as they come up against Moses' leadership. (See Numbers 14 KJV.) This epidiorthoo aspect of God is explored in some more depth in chapter 2 under the examination of God as punitive order.

THE ORDERS EXPERT

There are varying manifestations of our God who is order being, speaking, creating, acting as, commanding, fixing, arranging, restoring, and giving order. These are covered in the following chapters, but why does God want us to be orders experts? And what is an orders expert? The term 'orders expert' was dropped in my spirit the very first day I began writing and was novel to me until God started exploding in my spirit an understanding of what this concept meant. The God who is order makes orders in His divine role of arranging the world, He moves to dispel disorder and remove unruly behaviour in His house and among His people by making orders to restore order, Christians make orders daily when they pray, and orders are how we use our spiritual weapons to defeat the enemy. Christians issue orders, live by orders, and fight with orders, but do not clearly appreciate what they are doing. The issuing of spiritual orders is the vehicle through which Christians navigate life and from which they launch their missile attacks against the devil, yet they do not think of it in this manner.

An orders expert is a skilled spiritual warfare agent of God who is fully equipped with the understanding of what he is doing in battling the principalities and powers of darkness; he knows how to use spiritual orders with precision and refinement, and he is capable of invading and exiting enemy territory unseen to execute, devastate, and level the forces of darkness. Becoming an orders expert is an end-time requirement for engagement in spiritual warfare. Becoming an orders expert refers to the spiritual grooming, sharpening, refining, and perfecting of the skills of using warfare orders. It is about seeking increased discernment, knowledge, understanding, and training. It means first recognising and understanding who God is (order), who you are (a creation of order, for order, and to be order), the positioning from which you are to operate (spiritual authority realm), what you are doing (issuing spiritual orders), and that there are various types of orders to apply in warfare, so you must know them and know how to best utilise your God-given arsenal of spiritual weapons. Becoming an orders expert facilitates the believer in being better placed to become a more effective spiritual warrior. It starts off, however, with understanding and accepting that God is order.

CHAPTER 2

GOD IS ORDER

The nature of God is order. The first biblical statement is a declaratory pronouncement, the first biblical act is one of order, and the first biblical presentation of God is as creative order. (See Genesis 1:1–3 KJV.) If the very first three sentences in the Bible are formulated in terms of an order, then God, by this, is saying something to His people; He is saying, 'God is order.'[14] It was not by chance that when God spoke the world into order, He spoke using declaratory language: 'In the beginning God created the heaven and the earth' (Genesis 1:1 KJV). This declaration leaves no room for dispute; He is the Father of creation. In making this declaration, God was not changing anything; He was merely stating or affirming a truth. Another declaratory pronouncement that speaks to what was obtained at the beginning of time is to be found in the gospel of John: 'In the beginning was the Word, and the Word was with God, and the Word was God' (John 1:1 KJV).

This is a declaratory order being pronounced.[5] If both declarations of what was obtained at the beginning of time are read together, God is in effect saying of Himself that it is what it is; this pronouncement is unassailable, fixed, constant, immutable, unchangeable, undeniable, irreversible, incontestable, and untouchable. He is saying of the world that this is what it is to be – a creation of order, by order, and for order. He is saying of His Son that this is who He is; He is to have prominence over the world to affect order, represent Him as order, and be order. The declaration in the first sentence of the gospel of John speaks to the inseparable nature of God, the timelessness of God, and the centrality of the Word in the construct of the Godhead.

DECLARATORY ORDER

The opening declaratory statement used in Genesis is a pronouncement of God's creative power, invincibility, and sovereignty, and of the unity of the Godhead. Yes, the Godhead is referenced in the first three verses of Genesis: verse one presents God the creator; verse two shows the Holy Spirit in action, as the Water of life, and verse three presents the Son, who is the Light of the world. Within these first three verses, we are told of the darkness and void that existed and of the Spirit moving, and breathing life into the earth. These verses present God as order in all the various Greek meanings of the word; He is the diatasso, taxis, and epidiorthoo order wrapped up in one. By declaring He is the creator, God is in effect saying that He is ordering the world, acting as restorer of light and life, arranging and commanding order, appointing and giving order to things, breathing life into the elements, and setting things in order. In essence, God is order.

In a similar vein, the opening sentence used by God in the gospel of John is also a presentation of God as order. It consists of a string of declaratory orders representative of order. It establishes that the Word was in existence at the beginning, that the Word was operating with God, and that the Word was God. (See John 1:1 KJV.) The Word here is a direct reference to Jesus Christ, who is described as 'the Word' in the Bible: 'And the Word was made flesh, and dwelt among us, (and we beheld his glory, the glory as of the only begotten of the Father,) full of grace and truth' (John 1:14 KJV). This designation of Jesus Christ is also confirmed in Revelation when it states, 'And he was clothed with a vesture dipped in blood: and his name is called The Word of God' (Revelation 19:13 KJV). The expression 'the Word of God' signifies that this is how God communicates with humanity; through Jesus Christ, the Word manifests in the flesh. Here and throughout the Bible, Jesus is presented as the written Word, the spoken Word, the Word made flesh, the declarative Word, the creative Word, and the representative Word. In effect, the Word is order. Thus, by the opening sentence in the gospel of John, God Himself is not only reflected in those words as order, but the oneness and unity of God the Father, the Son and the Holy Spirit are depicted as entwined in that sentence. This first sentence in the gospel of John never held so much meaning to me as when the Holy Spirit began to allow it to explode in my spirit. It is crafted as a declaratory statement on purpose because it is meant to indicate that its essence is indisputable. It is a declaratory pronouncement of truth, with the truth being who God is – order.[6]

If God considered it significant enough to present Himself first as order, through the use of a declaratory order, before He even began the creation process, then why has the concept of God as order been buried, unappreciated; de-emphasised; and not spoken about in His church? Why has the knowledge of and experience of God as order been relegated to the fringes of the church world and not taken a central place? Why has it not been preached about more frequently or been used as the yardstick to measure and guide the Christian walk? Can it be that the solution for many of the ills beleaguering the church lies in this failure to place order as a primary principle in our lives and in the church? Why was it so important to God to present Himself as order, as the beginning biblical principle, and why craft it as a declaration? I felt a nudge in my spirit that the use of the declaratory form was meant to indicate that this truth of God as order is incontestable and irrefutable. It was also an indicator that the converse of God being order is Satan being disorder, which also is a truth that is unchallengeable. It meant that from the very beginning, when order presented or when God introduced Himself as declaratory order, disorder would have emerged and sought to be prevalent on the earth. In fact, the 'darkness and void' in Genesis were representative of the disorder against which order presented.

It was at this point that I understood the importance of God presenting not just as any order but as declaratory order, which is the unchallengeable, undeniable, unassailable, and immutable truth of who He is. This was meant to indicate that God is the order against which Satan, as disorder, cannot stand or win. It was an untouchable truth and an avowal of who God is, establishing and affirming the incontestability of God's nature as order. In other words, order is the standard against which disorder, the principal demonic spirit unleashed against mankind, could not prevail. As this understanding was poured into me, it became clear why the revelation of God as order had hitherto been shrouded in darkness and why it needed to emerge in the light and be given clarity in these last days. The importance of God presenting this revelation that He is order, in the form of a declaration, became clear; for this truth was absolute and unquestionable. Moreover, it was the functional mode that man was required to operate in at this time.

What is meant by man being required to function in the declaratory mode? Simply, if God operates in the declaratory realm, then as a Christian, you are required also to function in this realm, as a core source of who you are. To achieve this and so operate effectively in declaratory authority, you must do so with an understanding of what that means and of the power wielded at that level to affect the heavens and to make the kingdom of darkness scatter. When you speak from that declaratory level with the clear understanding of what your impact is and what you are doing, the enemy is dissipated and rendered silent and must bow in acknowledgement of the truth contained in your words. Walking in declarative authority is no simple matter. And it is not as simple as using declarations to try to bring change to vexing issues that keep plaguing or tormenting your life. In fact, many Christians use declarations as a matter of course in their prayer lives with the intention of bringing about change but without a clear understanding of the purpose and power of walking in declarative authority.

When you speak with declarative authority, you assert, pronounce, affirm, or avow the truth of a thing. It is not about trying to change the truth, but that truth is to manifest as what it is. So when you pray, declaring that your circumstances will change, or pleading with and warning the devil to let go, that is not exercising declarative authority. You walk in declarative authority by proclaiming the truth over your circumstances and directing a speedy manifestation of that truth in the corporeal realm. Let us look at an example of a declaratory utterance you can make: 'I am a child of the Most High God, and I have the power of the Holy Spirit within me; therefore, Satan, I pronounce you a defeated foe, crushed and trampled under my shoe heel, and so you must flee from me in the name of Jesus Christ. You have no power to prevail in this or any other situation in my life. The victory over this situation is already handed to me by Jesus Christ and it is mine, not yours, to celebrate.' The truth contained in these declarations is unassailable and immutable, and because it cannot be shaken or contested, the enemy must flee in the face of your declarative authority. This alone suffices for it to be so; it is about releasing and pronouncing what is or unveiling its existence. Walking in declarative authority is not about declaring that your situation will change from one of defeat to victory; it is about accepting and asserting that you are the winner by Jesus Christ (declarative truth) and that Satan is your already-defeated foe. It is about changing your perspective and declaration on the situation. So your perception of the thing must be how you see it (its true source) before and while making the declaration. It is like the Genesis declaration that 'God created the heaven and the earth' – there is no alternative perception there; it is what it is. This Genesis declarative statement was made and affirmed as truth even before the actual creation process started.

Similarly, when you are walking in declarative authority, you perceive the pronouncement for the truth of what it is and assert its truthfulness as what is. There is no room for doubt, dispute, or questioning when making a declaration or when walking in this level of authority. And certainly, it is not about praying for your circumstances to change but about affirming the truth over your situation. You must see truth, feel it, taste it, hear it, and believe it. Truth must be a sensory reality in your prayer to the point at which it is actualized in the physical realm. If you are making declarations in your prayer without this understanding and from this positioning, then you may very well be speaking in denial, dispute, and doubt without realising it. I have elaborated below on declaratory orders, but suffice it to say that declaratory authority is most powerful if it is understood and applied correctly by the intercessory Christian and every other believer.

There are many instances where God shows up as declaratory order in the Bible. Order speaks of authority, and sometimes, God presents or operates as declaratory authority or creative authority or as some other aspect of authority. The Bible is replete with examples of God operating in declaratory power and pronouncing these types of orders. As a Christian, learning to recognise and understand this declaratory aspect of God will sharpen your operationalized use of this power in these last days and make you an unassailable spiritual force with which to contend. This declaratory aspect of God is seen most graphically where there is disorder, for He emerges in declaratory or creative authority as order. For instance, this is the Genesis manifestation of God. He also showed up as declaratory order when the Ten Commandments were handed down to Israel: 'I am the LORD thy God, which have brought thee out of the land of Egypt, out of the house of bondage. Thou shalt have no other gods before me' (Exodus 20:2–3 KJV). The force and power enclosed in these words are indisputable; it is what it is.

Yet another declaratory statement by God is 'I am Alpha and Omega, the beginning and the ending, ... which is, and which was, and which is to come, the Almighty' (Revelation 1:8 KJV). Its use in the final book in the Bible is not only apt but is also a powerful proclamation of all that God is – the Almighty and Great I Am. He shows up in the beginning as the creator of order, and in the ending, He will manifest as the restorer of order. Declaratory order is the most powerful and sacrosanct manifestation of the authority of God.

CREATIVE ORDER

If the first pronouncement of God was a declaratory order, then it is understandable why God will move next to issuing a creative order. A creative order is a type of declaratory order in action. It demonstrates the power contained in the declaratory order but goes a step further to action the truth, or to put the affirmed truth into operation. So in the beginning was creative order, operationalized and on full display. Everything was geared towards life, growth, health, creativity, success, and victory. This is the creative authority that a Christian is required to walk in and demonstrate daily. It means that our words, actions, thoughts, and relationships should manifest creativity and life. Instead, Christians are speaking in a language of qualification, caveat, exception, negativity, and destruction, as if it were their primary tongue. What is unfortunate about this is that Christians do not even recognise when they are speaking this language of qualification or the regularity of its use. Even when it is pointed out to believers, they continue, unabashed and unconcerned, with the loose use and misuse of their tongues, as if they are incapable of exercising control over this body part. I call it the new 'first tongue' of the modern Christian – the language of disqualification and disentitlement to live creative and victorious lives. It is the converse of the power that God has called believers to exercise or walk in as a natural and normal aspect of their Christian living.

Most Christians know or have heard about the power of the tongue and are aware that this power is creative. But do you know that if this power is misused, it can be destructive? Yet we persist in using our tongues in mindless and destructive ways:

> Even so the tongue is a little member, and boasteth great things. Behold, how great a matter a little fire kindleth! And the tongue is a fire, a world of iniquity: so is the tongue among our members, that it defileth the whole body, and setteth on fire the course of nature; and it is set on fire of hell. For every kind of beasts, and of birds, and of serpents, and of things in the sea, is tamed, and hath been tamed of mankind: But the tongue can no man tame; it is an unruly evil, full of deadly poison. Therewith bless we God, even the Father; and therewith curse we men, which are made after the similitude of God. Out of the same mouth proceedeth blessing and cursing. My brethren, these things ought not so to be. (James 3:5–10 KJV)

The God who is order is calling His children to walk in creative authority. Walking in creative authority involves operating in the realm of breathing new life into dead situations, similar to the power displayed in the valley of dead bones. (See Ezekiel 37:1–14 KJV.) It is about walking in resurrection authority, which is life giving and renewing. It is instructive to note that the obedience of Ezekiel to the command of God led to life being infused into these dead bones. God wants His children to walk in 'Ezekiel obedience' and speak life to the dead situations in and around us and to stop appropriating unto ourselves death through our tongues. To do this, we must stop walking in denial of this lethal use of our creative power 'the tongue' and recognise that its misuse barricades us from walking in victory.

Walking in creative authority also involves issuing orders that will dispel darkness or fill the void represented by darkness. Your darkness may be diseases; joblessness; homelessness; barrenness; a lack of finances; feelings of rejection, oppression, or depression; or any number of attacks, but understand that you are vested with the creative authority to speak life into these areas of void. That is the same creative power that lies in the Word, whom we accepted as Lord and Saviour, so we have it within us to function at that level of creativity. Remember that God is order, creative order, which means He is in the business of breathing life into dead situations, arranging and setting things in order, and restoring order. Three renowned examples of creative order, where life was breathed into dead situations and the revival power of God was displayed, include the resurrection of the widow's son by Elijah, the resurrection of the son of the widow of Nain, and the miracle performed on Jairus' daughter. (See 1 Kings 17:10–24; Luke 7:11–15; and Mark 5:22–43 KJV.) In one of these instances, the deceased person was actually on his way to be buried when creative order turned up and upset the plan of man by reversing the death edict. In all cases, it shows creative order in operation to restore life and order, even in the face of death.

PUNITIVE ORDER

God is order, including punitive order, so He must function as such in His interactions with mankind, reproving and chastising us for our benefit so that we may be partakers of eternal life. The Bible states, 'My son, despise not thou the chastening of the Lord, nor faint when thou art rebuked of him: For whom the Lord loveth he chasteneth, and scourgeth every son whom he receiveth' (Hebrews 12:5–6 KJV). This aspect of God as punitive order is seen not only in His dealings with believers but also with unbelievers. There are many functional manifestations of God as punitive order throughout the Bible. One such instance is where there is disobedience to God's rules and orders, whether in the personal lives of believers or in the church or world at large. In such cases, God operates as punitive order, chastising and correcting sin, whether committed by believers or evildoers who do not serve Him. This manifestation of God as punitive order is His response to acts of disobedience or breaches of His order, and not necessarily because of immorality, although there are many cases where immorality is punished.

One such example of God as punitive order occurs in the Old Testament when Korah, Dathan, and Abiram, three believers who were ministers before God in the tabernacle but possessed rebellious and disobedient spirits, plotted to overthrow God's order. These conspirators introduced disorder against God's order by trying to supplant Moses and Aaron's leadership through the questioning of their claim to holiness and their entitlement to the positions they held. They disapproved of Moses' supreme authority in civil matters, and of Aaron and his family having the exclusive privileges of the priesthood, because Korah and his company of collaborators felt that they were being unjustly confined to the 'inferior service' of the tabernacle. They accused Moses and Aaron of usurping privileges and offices rightfully belonging to others, of presenting themselves only as holy when all of God's people were holy, and of inciting the people of God to rise up against them. Moses sought to reason with them that it was not 'a small thing' or inconsequential for these three men, and the other 'leaders of the congregation' joined with them, to be appointed by God to serve in His tabernacle and minister to the congregation. Yet still they wanted more, so they unleashed a full-scale rebellion. They refused to be obedient to Moses' directives, murmured against him, and accused him of bringing them out of a land that was flowing with milk and honey to kill them in the wilderness. (See Numbers 16 KJV.) For their rebellion against God's ordained structure, organisation, and established order, God caused the earth to swallow them and everything belonging to them, including their children and grandchildren, and a fire consumed their 250 associates:

> But if the LORD make a new thing, and the earth open her mouth, and swallow them up, with all that appertain unto them, and they go down quick into the pit; then ye shall understand that these men have provoked the LORD. And it came to pass, as he had made an end of speaking all these words, that the ground clave asunder that was under them: And the earth opened her mouth, and swallowed them up, and their houses, and all the men that appertained unto Korah, and all their goods. They, and all that appertained to them, went down alive into the pit, and the earth closed upon them: and they perished from among the congregation. (Numbers 16:30–33 KJV)

Despite this powerful display of God's judgment and punitive authority, the congregants continued with their stance of disobedience and defiance. On the very next day, the congregation was unrelenting in its disorderly, disobedient conduct by actively opposing Moses and Aaron and objecting to this act of discipline. When they again gathered against Moses and Aaron, accusing them of killing God's people, the presence of the Lord came and covered the tabernacle, and His glory appeared, causing a plague to kill 14,700 of them. (See Numbers 16:41–50 KJV.) These were two instances in which the sin was not immorality; it was rebellion and opposition to the order of God for divinely structuring His congregation, which caused Him to manifest as punitive order and to issue death sentences on His own people. Korah typifies the presumptuous and self-seeking 'leader' who was appointed to serve in the tabernacle but who wanted the priesthood, which was more than God had purposed for his life. When he did not get his way, he was willing to operate outside of God's purpose, breaching God's order.

There are many 'Korahs' within and outside of the church who are puffed up, arrogant, self-promoting, and disobedient and who see no impropriety in challenging God's order. These Korahs feel entitled to and justified in putting themselves forward for spiritual promotion, outside of God's plans for their lives. Such people will step on anyone in their way to propel themselves, but when God turns up, He upsets the plans of man. Sometimes, as Christians, we are dissatisfied with serving in lower-level leadership positions, ignoring the benefits that can come from grooming for a higher position. This may result in us electing to speak ill of or murmur against our spiritual heads or even, as Korah did, to rise up in rebellion and disobedience and so facilitate the spirit of disorder to emerge in the midst of God's sanctuary. You are to be cognizant, however, that your defiance and disobedience may be the channels for disorder but that the God of the sanctuary and your life is order and His purpose will prevail. 'Many are the plans in a person's heart, but it is the LORD's purpose that prevails' (Proverbs 19:21 NIV). It is interesting to note here that disobedience and disorder, which led to this revolt, did not stop the high priesthood of Aaron from being confirmed. It serves to show that in the face of defiance, disobedience, revolt, and disorder, God will turn up as diatasso and epidiorthoo order to set things right. (See Numbers 17 KJV.)

Another example where disorder stepped in, causing a violation of God's order for worship attracting an execution order to be issued by God, was with Nadab and Abihu, the sons of Aaron. They were both appointed, along with their father and two other brothers, to be priests of God, and He had given clear instructions as to the conduct of worship before Him. Instead of obeying God, they operated in disobedience by breaching His instructions and offering incense using a 'strange' fire rather than the fire taken from the incense that burned perpetually on the altar. By defying God's clear instructions on how worship was to be done, His anger was kindled against them. In response to their act of disobedience and disorder, God sent fire from heaven and devoured them, striking them dead before the sanctuary. Yet again, the sin in this case was not an act of gross immorality but a defilement and desecration of His sanctuary and disobedience to His instructions on worship that caused God to move swiftly to reinstate order. This punitive act of a death sentence was meant to ensure that worship remains pure and undefiled and that He will continue to be glorified in true holiness. (See Leviticus 10:1–3 KJV; Numbers 3:4 KJV.) It goes to show that there is an order to worship and to prayer – especially in the house of God – and He guards that order jealously. Thus, any act that goes against God's preordained order equates to disorder and can bring punishment from God. 'God is a Spirit: and they that worship him must worship him in spirit and in truth' (John 4:24 KJV). It shows that God is serious about order and that any form of disorder or disobedience will provoke a response from Him to restore order.

Another pertinent example of God turning up to correct disorder or disobedience occurred when Uzzah transported the ark of the covenant on a new cart instead of having the Levites carry it by its poles. When the oxen stumbled and Uzzah touched the ark in error, God killed him. (See 2 Samuel 6:1–11 KJV.) This execution order was issued yet again for non-compliance with an order of God and not gross immorality. We see another such example in God refusing to allow Moses to enter Canaan because he smote the rock to produce water from it instead of speaking to it as God had instructed. (See Numbers 20:1–13 KJV.) The punishment in this case was not an execution order but an exclusion or debarment order.

Another case of disobedience of the Word of God that caused a death sentence from God involved the unnamed prophet of God who healed King Jeroboam and then disobeyed God's order not to eat or drink anything in that place. When he defied God's order and ate and drank, albeit through trickery, he was punished for his disobedience by death. (See 1 Kings 13 KJV.) Yet another illustration of disobedience occurred when Lot's wife was turned into a pillar of salt when she looked back, breaching God's directive not to do so, as they escaped from Sodom. (See Genesis 19:17–26 KJV.) Here again, an execution order was issued to deal with this act of disobedience.

ARRANGING ORDER

Incorporated in the definition of order is the act of 'arranging', or 'an arrangement', which aptly describes how God acts in various circumstances. The word 'arranging' refers to how God operates to put things in order; it is a continual aspect of His functioning as order in the world. An integral part of God as order is seen in His arranging or designing His sanctuary. This is exemplified in the tabernacle of Exodus. (See Exodus 25 KJV.) God gave detailed and specific instructions for the building and outfitting of His tabernacle to ensure that everything was set in order. This included clear instructions on the offerings and sacrifices to be provided, the furniture, the utensils, the various coverings for the tabernacle, the dimensions for the inner and outer courts, the dimensions for the entire tabernacle area, the methods used to make the various curtains and coverings, and even the techniques used to make the clothes for the high priest and other members of the priesthood. After all these instructions were given, they were required to be completed before Aaron and his sons were consecrated for the ministry of the tabernacle. This arranging aspect of God's order is seen throughout the Bible as He operates to bring about order, put things in order, and resolve disputes.

JUDICIAL ORDER

'For the LORD is our judge, the LORD is our lawgiver, the LORD is our king; he will save us' (Isaiah 33:22 KJV). God is judicial order; it is an integral part of His nature and function as the God who is order. He is the ultimate judge and dispenser of divine justice; these positions are linked to and are outflows of His purity, holiness, righteousness, and separation from sin. God's justice, or function as judicial order, is something that is directly communicable to man. The Bible is chock-full of examples of God operating as a judge to dispense order and divine justice, and His call to believers to operate in that spiritual realm is explored in detail in chapters 5 and 6 of this book. Suffice it to say that an innate part of the nature of God is justice and that He operates in this capacity to bring about order, to resolve disputes, and to arrange things in order. When God is operating as punitive order, it is also an aspect of His function as judicial order. Judicial order is a wider umbrella term that encompasses punitive order but also speaks to God operating as compensatory order or as the upholder of justice. When God is operating in His compensatory mode, He is rewarding and recompensing His children, not issuing punishment. He is still judicial order and operating as the Holy Judge but is functioning to issue rewards. The duality of His functioning as punitive and compensatory order will be seen on the day of the great Judgment of mankind. (See Revelation 20:12 KJV.)

In the interim, there are many biblical examples of God as judicial compensatory order, with one being the story of Joseph, who was dumped into a well and then sold into slavery by his siblings. (See Genesis 37.)

God overruled the ill done to Joseph and used the same circumstances meant for evil towards him to bring him into a place of largesse. God caused him to be favoured by the Egyptians and placed him in a position where, in a time of scarcity, he was the instrument used to supply the wants of Egypt and the surrounding nations:

> And the LORD was with Joseph, and he was a prosperous man; and he was in the house of his master the Egyptian. And his master saw that the LORD was with him, and that the LORD made all that he did to prosper in his hand. And Joseph found grace in his sight, and he served him: and he made him overseer over his house, and all that he had he put into his hand ... that the LORD blessed the Egyptian's house for Joseph's sake; and the blessing of the LORD was upon all that he had in the house, and in the field. (Genesis 39:2–5 KJV)

From an alternative perspective, a large part of God being judicial order is seen in His dispensing of orders. In fact, orders are how justice is dispensed in the earthly realm to set things in order – hence the centrality of their use in spiritual warfare. This is no surprise, as the character of God is order. In His judicial functioning as order, God is seen exercising divine correction and chastisement of believers. (See 1 Corinthians 11:31–32

KJV.) But it is also seen in God issuing rewards to His people and promoting this reward-giving aspect of His nature. 'And, behold, I come quickly; and my reward is with me, to give every man according as his work shall be' (Revelation 22:12 KJV). This facet of God is also seen in Jeremiah 31:9–17 KJV. Pertinent to this is the following scriptural excerpt:

> Then shall the virgin rejoice in the dance, both young men and old together: for I will turn their mourning into joy, and will comfort them, and make them rejoice from their sorrow. And I will satiate the soul of the priests with fatness, and my people shall be satisfied with my goodness, saith the LORD. Thus saith the LORD; A voice was heard in Ramah, lamentation, and bitter weeping; Rahel weeping for her children refused to be comforted for her children, because they were not. Thus saith the LORD; Refrain thy voice from weeping, and thine eyes from tears: for thy work shall be rewarded, saith the LORD; and they shall come again from the land of the enemy. (Jeremiah 31:13–16 KJV)

A CALL TO ORDER: WHY GOD RELATES TO MAN AS ORDER

The above discussion on God as declaratory, creative, arranging, punitive, compensatory, and judicial order seeks to give a cursory glimpse into the varying manifestations of God as order but does not seek to assume that they are the only forms of Him operating as order. In fact, these are just five ways in which He shows up as order against disorder. However, as order, God also acts as the upholder of order or as vindicatory order (that is, to defend, assert, or prove the rights of those wronged) or even as exemplary order (that is, to set standards to follow or send a message to the disobedient that his actions are not tolerated). No one can limit God or box Him into operating in any predetermined or fixed way, and in fact, the scriptures are filled with many other instances of God as order, as He seeks to equip His people to become better and more effective in spiritual warfare and to become partakers of eternal life. Above are but a few instances where God is seen operationalising as order, so as to give context for the discussion below on becoming an orders expert. It is certainly not an exhaustive list of ways in which He manifests as order. It also serves as the platform for understanding why God is calling on believers to relate to Him as order in these final days. For if God can show up as various forms of order (declaratory, creative, punitive, compensatory, etc.) and use orders in warring against the evil forces of darkness (creative, declaratory, punitive, or execution orders, etc.), then His call to us to see Him as order and to become orders experts is meaningful in such a context. With this small insight into God as order, I hope that the door is now cracked for increased revelation on this aspect of His nature and character to unfold.

It is important to understand why God wants to relate to man as order, for the call to order is critical to this period in time, when mankind is being ushered headlong towards the end-time collision with disorder. It is a call to His church to walk in the revelation that He is order and allow Him to relate to you as order, to enable you to live lives of order and so that you can become trained in being orders experts in spiritual warfare. It is a call to be like Him – to reach for perfection. The call to order is a call to come to God Himself, for He is order, and a call to marshal your spiritual weapons against Satan, the source and father of disorder. It means that you are called to image God and to operate as an orders expert.

In becoming orders experts, you are to be aware that, while disorder existed following the creation of the world and while mankind's disobedience (initially and since the Genesis period) was birthed out of disorder's prevalence on the earth, God was always order. Further, the battle to regain order in the believer's life starts with obedience to the call of the God who is order. God needs to relate to man as order so that mankind will understand the importance of being and imaging order in his personal life and Christian walk, as well as fine tuning his use of spiritual orders in the final battle with disorder. It covers also His church as being or becoming order (His image) and using order to prepare for the return of its Lord and Saviour, Jesus Christ.

CHAPTER 3

ORDER IN THE CHURCH

The issue of order in the church is clothed with sensitivity but must be treated honestly and fairly if the body is to realise growth and move into perfection. A church is the house of God and thus typifies order. To put this another way, the house of God is a house of order. What constitutes order is not subject to qualification or personal preferences; order is an immutable and unchangeable concept. Order is who God is; it is an intrinsic and indelible part of His nature, and His church is called to be order and walk in order. There is no allowance for different standards to reflect order; it is simply what it is. It is a concept that cannot be qualified, adjusted, varied, or amended to suit whichever denominational church is being focused on to determine whether it is represented there. Immaterial are the name of the church and the movement of God that gave birth to that church, as well as whether it is headed by an apostolic, evangelic, prophetic, healing, or teaching anointing. Those realities do not determine what order is or whether it exists in the body.

The measuring stick for what constitutes order and the test tubes for revealing its existence are incapable of manipulation or gerrymandering to give false results. What is order is already fixed. It is much like God. It cannot be explained away by stating, 'Well, the Holy Spirit is in control here, so that explains the disorder.' That argument is fallacious, false, erroneous, and contrary to the Word of God because the Holy Spirit is part of the godhead; He cannot bring, represent, or be disorder. It is blasphemous to even try to justify the existence of disorder in the body by hiding behind the cover of the Holy Spirit. It is impossible for the Holy Spirit to be or manifest as disorder.

THE UNRULY CHURCH

'For God is not a God of disorder, but of peace – as in all the congregations of the Lord's people' (1 Corinthians 14:33 NIV).

God is calling on His church in these last days to embrace, walk in, reflect, speak, pray, and be order. Just as God is order, His church must be the image of order. We are called to present as perfect in Christ Jesus, which is not an aspirational impossibility but is a reality for which the church must strive. The word 'perfect' as used here is equivalent to the Greek '*teleion*', which means 'whole, complete, or mature' and implies an ethical perfection or flawless behaviour.[7] It does not mean 'incapable of doing wrong'; nor does it imply that the flesh will stop warring with your spirit man. In fact, ethical perfection suggests that when faced with temptations, your choice will always be the principled, fitting, proper, virtuous, and just one. (See Romans 7 KJV.) As a believer in Christ, is your choice always principled, proper, ethical, objective, fair, and just, or do you take shelter behind the mantra that no one is or can be perfect, in order to assuage or soften your guilty feelings about your unprincipled choices? When last did you honestly examine your choices (and not the choices of others) to find out if they line up with what God would have you do or say in a particular situation?

Being perfect points to having a mature relationship with God in which the believer is fully committed to Him and seeks to do His will. It refers to a relationship in which the believer's lifestyle mirrors love, forgiveness, humility, and order – God. It starts with His people, who are called by His name, engaging in truthful introspection to find out if order exists in His church and in the lives of the individual members of the church. Where order does not exist, it requires that believers cry out for and implement it as a central principle in His body.

The spirit of disorder operating in His church is

nothing new, for it manifested in the church at Corinth, and the apostle Paul spoke out against this:

> Now I beseech you, brethren, by the name of our Lord Jesus Christ, that ye all speak the same thing, and that there be no divisions among you; but that ye be perfectly joined together in the same mind and in the same judgment. For it hath been declared unto me of you, my brethren, by them which are of the house of Chloe, that there are contentions among you. (1 Corinthians 1:10–11 KJV)

Even Jesus Christ had to take steps to disrupt disorder in His temple in a bid to restore order. (See John 2:13–22 KJV and Matthew 21:12–17 KJV.) So the end-time church is not immune from the infiltration of disorder in the body. In fact, the spirit of disorder has never ceased operating among and against God's people or God's order.

In these final days, disorder is manifesting with a greater force and intensity and with a heightened drive to succeed in its mission. So the fact that disorder is pervasive in the body does not surprise. It becomes dangerous not when it is seeping into or is present in the body but rather when we operate in denial of it, allow it to become a normalised part of church life, and then walk in complete blindness to its existence. In some churches, disorder is so entrenched, so set in concrete, and so prevalent that it is no longer perceived as disorder. This blinding display of disorder is not a new manifestation; it may take various forms, but its mission is clear and focuses on shutting down and shuttering man's senses to order. But its manner of operating has always been exposed; it is constantly being called out and condemned for its attack on man's visual, auditory, and other senses. In one biblical instance, it was described thus: 'Son of man, thou dwellest in the midst of a rebellious house, which have eyes to see, and see not; they have ears to hear, and hear not: for they are a rebellious house' (Ezekiel 12:2 KJV).

Disorder in the church is fortified and encouraged by the demonic spirit of gradualism, which moves slowly and imperceptibly in the world to cause untruths, false doctrines, and sin to become normalised and acceptable. Gradualism is 'a spectacled spirit'; it walks around placing dark shades on mankind, preventing clear vision and giving the impression to believers that they are being progressive and hip in their perception of sin. Sin, seen through the lens of gradualism, is excused and accepted rather than rejected. You only have to look around at what is happening in the world to see how 'sin' is gradually being qualified and presented as acceptable, normal, and no longer as sin. But the God who is order is moving to take corrective steps to expose it and weed it out. His intent is to purge and sanitise His house, for He is not returning for a church of disorder. Those who will fight against this new wave of order, who will not yield and submit to order, and who think this teaching is not applicable to them will find themselves trampled upon and their resistance whipped into subjection to the Word of God.

The prevalence of disorder in the unruly church is not only linked to the demonic spirit of gradualism but is tied also to the clear choice by many spiritual heads not to offend. You may ask why it is that what obtains today in many churches is disorder. Why has the church been wearing spiritual blinders about God as order and about the need for order in the house of God? As time progresses, order in the church has become more and more of a foreign, obscure, and elusive concept, by choice. This explains why disorder has not attracted rebuke (as Paul swiftly bestowed upon the church at Corinth), condemnation, or even comment; we proceed as if it were not evident or deserving of correction. It seems that many ministers are willing to sacrifice order at the table of a ballooning membership. They try not to offend relationships, so they ignore bad reports about congregants rather than issue swift reprimands and condemnation. This type of soft approach to pastoring has allowed disorder to become the prevailing spirit in the church world rather than order. I call it the 'Eli phenomenon'; where the response to unruly, offensive behaviour in church is met with a slight tap on the wrist and is effectively a non-response. This is a deadly and risky approach to pastoring. But disorder is now being exposed for what it is; for it cannot remain undisturbed in a house of order – His church. It is being identified and called out as the unwanted, disruptive, demonic attack on the church that it really is.

The unruly church is being called to return to order. It is only for so long that a God who is order will abide an unruly church. Something has to be seriously wrong where the head of a congregation can remain mute in the face of disorder, operate in denial of it, deal with it softly, or excuse unruly conduct as allowing the Holy Spirit to have His way. And I am not referring here to when the Spirit is moving during a service and His power is on full display. Order cannot survive in disorder – especially where that disruptive conduct is manifesting in the house of God, in the midst of His presence. God will move to sanitise His church; He will reprimand and restore order and wipe off the Eli spirit as He did previously. (See 1 Samuel 2:22–34; 3:13–14; and 4 KJV.)

The story of Eli is an apt illustration of how God who is order responds to disorder in His church. Eli, whose sons, Hophni and Phinehas, were being disorderly in the temple of God, had failed to reprimand them sternly and suffered the ultimate punishment of having his generation wiped out. The Bible speaks of Hophni and Phinehas as behaving so outrageously and disorderly that they attracted deep disgust among the people and brought the services of the temple into odium in the people's eyes. They were even engaged in sexual lasciviousness, and this was made known to Eli. 'Now Eli was very old, and heard all that his sons did unto all Israel; and how they lay with the women that assembled at the door of the tabernacle of the congregation' (1 Samuel 2:22 KJV). Yet Eli, the Lord's priest, treated this bad report lightly. Apart from this glaring paternal inaction and administrative stumble, there was no indication that Eli lacked faith in God or was anything but careful in the administration of God's affairs. In fact, he operated as a devoted high priest and was the first judge of priestly descent of Israel for forty years. His misstep was that he chose to give a mild and ineffective scolding to his sons rather than acting swiftly, as required of a priest, to harness and eliminate the unruly behaviour with a severe and forceful rebuke. (See 1 Samuel 2:12–17, 22 KJV.) In effect, Eli allowed his parental love to hinder him from exercising proper corrective authority over his sons, to his detriment and that of his lineage. Similarly, an unruly church upsets the orderly constitution of Our Heavenly Father and attracts judgment. 'For the time is come that judgment must begin at the house of God: and if it first begin at us, what shall the end be of them that obey not the gospel of God?' (1 Peter 4:17 KJV).

ORDER IN CHURCH LEADERSHIP

Being appointed to a leadership position in the church is not a licence to walk in disorder but a call to order. (See 1 Timothy 3:1–13 KJV.) There is a personal responsibility on the part of leaders to exemplify order, which is effectively demonstrating in their lives that God is order. Leaders in the church are the standard-bearers of order as the stewards of God. Apart from their personal mandate, they also represent order in their leadership roles in the church and are charged with the responsibility to uphold and maintain it. Put another way, leaders function to pilot, steer, and guide the believers on their spiritual journeys and must monitor and guard against malfunctioning in the body, whether personally or in the body of Christ.

The onus is on the church leadership, as the conduit of order, to live orderly and exemplary lives if they are to instil order in the sanctuary. A disorderly sanctuary is reflective of its leadership. Disorderly leadership filters down and pollutes the sanctuary, affecting the governance and structure of the house of God. Where the lives of its leadership are in disarray or in the clutches of disorder, this militates against the existence of order in the body. As an elder or bishop in your church, your life and relationships must be reflective of order, not disorder. It is stated unequivocally that 'if a man know not how to rule his own house, how shall he take care of the church of God?' (1 Timothy 3:5 KJV). Those involved in ministry as bishops and leaders are called to walk blamelessly before God, not controlled by their own self-will, and to instil order in the church of God. It is written: 'For a bishop must be blameless, as the steward of God; not self-willed, not soon angry, not given to wine, no striker, not given to filthy lucre; But a lover of hospitality, a lover of good men, sober, just, holy, temperate; Holding fast the faithful word as he hath been taught, that he may be able by sound doctrine both to exhort and to convince the gainsayers' (Titus 1:7–9 KJV).

Order in leadership also takes into account the structure and governance of the church, the appointment to leadership, and the need to ensure that there is a healthy respect for the established order. The governing structure of the body of Christ was put in place to ensure order in presentation, in reporting, in guiding, and in controlling the Christian walk and conduct. Where there is disorder in the church, whether in the preaching of heresy or in a lack of respect for our elders and leaders, we are instructed to return to order – to set in place a structure of order and remove disorderly conduct by setting right again what is defective or that which has fallen into disorder. This is stated clearly: 'For this cause left I thee in Crete, that thou shouldest set in order the things that are wanting, and ordain elders in every city, as I had appointed thee' (Titus 1:5–16 KJV).

The instilling of a governing structure in the church is purposed to influence and build a system of order so disorder will not be able to abide in God's sanctuary. This is why placing persons in leadership positions in any church is a serious undertaking by any head and must be carried out prayerfully. In fact, the appointment of elders, bishops, and other leaders in the church is not an arbitrary practice but is a necessary step for instilling order. This responsibility to appoint leaders must, therefore, not be treated glibly but with the guidance of the Holy Spirit. Many churches have a basic structure for organising their leadership, with most comprising elders, deacons, board members, prayer ministry leaders, youth leaders, praise and worship leaders, and so on. It is incumbent on the apostolic and pastoral heads to fill leadership positions with members having the spiritual maturity, commitment, and faithfulness for the office in which there is a vacancy.

It is never recommended that pastors strive to show completeness in their leadership teams by sacrificing devoted, right standing, and orderly members for those who may be spiritually unqualified and bereft of commitment to God and the ministry. Remember that church leaders are conduits of order and presenters of God when they function in ministry. Degrees, holders of high offices in secular bodies, and wealth and class are not prerequisites for appointments as leaders in the church, for God is not influenced by man's position or title in life. 'For the LORD your God is God of gods, and Lord of lords, a great God, a mighty, and a terrible, which regardeth not persons, nor taketh reward' (Deuteronomy 10:17 KJV). It is incumbent on the apostolic and pastoral heads to avoid hastily, and without prayerful consideration, placing persons in leadership positions based on how they present in the secular circles. In the sectarian world, they may be ill equipped to represent our God who is order and can trigger numerous fallouts in the church, including a mass exodus in the number of congregants, facilitating the prevalence of disorder and hindering the work of God. A few truly dedicated, spiritually mature, and godly men and women of any class will trump a circle of spiritually thin 'pastoral ego boosters' as leaders any day.

Congregants are to be cautioned also that once leadership appointments are made, order dictates that respect be shown to your leaders and that dislike of a particular leader does not qualify as a valid excuse for changing where you fellowship. The disorderly spirit you leave with will just enter your new house of worship, for order is not applicable only to leaders but also to congregants. If, as a congregant without a leadership position, you are the purveyor of a disorderly spirit, it goes wherever you go. In some cases, this practice of flitting from church to church in condemnation of the disorder of your last place of worship and under the guise that you are being led by the Holy Spirit makes you a channel of disorder. Bear in mind that God is order and so is into replicating order on earth, and similarly, the devil operates by breeding and spreading disorder in various places of worship. A disorderly, disobedient, and self-righteous congregant is a ripe candidate through which this can be achieved.

ORDER IN THE SERVICE

A church that has order reflects God. It is not the only representation of God, but it is a primary one. Conversely, a church of disorder is a misrepresentation of God. It is easy to determine if a church is not concerned with manifesting order or is about disorder; just walk in on a Saturday or Sunday morning fifteen minutes before service is carded to start and watch the activities as they unfold. The spiritual maturity of a church can be gleaned from how far along on the continuum of order it is operating. And this does not mean that a church where 'the order of service' is fixed, robotic, and stifling the Holy Spirit represents order. This is not what order is, and in fact, it is representative of the imposition of the hand of man working to imprint his self-will on what really should be influenced by and ordered by the Holy Spirit. It is, in effect, a form of disorder.

Have you ever attended a church service where there is no order and a seeming lack of interest in presenting as order? The first message received by a visitor to any church service comes not from the pulpit. It is sent by the members' manner of conduct in receiving or greeting attendees and by what is on display before the service starts. If a church service is fixed to commence at 9:00 a.m. and at that time the musicians are hustling in, the microphone is being tested, people are milling around chatting, some are on their mobiles, others are having a quick breakfast, and there is no vested interest in showing respect for the house of God, this is not order. A prompt start of service sends the message that this congregation appreciates and respects order and understands that order represents God.

If the God you serve is order, then it starts with every single member of the church walking in and representing order. There are some churches where, as soon as the service starts, the members begin to walk about, whether on bathroom breaks, to take mobile calls, or to congregate outside the washroom area to chat. It disturbs and distracts when people are walking about during service or taking mobile calls, and what is more, it sends a strong message that this church lacks order and is disrespectful of God. It is also not reflective of order to have members eating and drinking in the sanctuary while service is in progress. And yes, your entrenched practice of sipping on water during service is reflective of disorder. A burgeoning practice is the use of mobiles to play video games during service. There is a need for proper telephone etiquette to be taught to and exercised by congregants, many of whom operate as if a failure to take a telephone call during service will cause a major catastrophic event.

Equally representative of disorder is members sitting during worship. If it were possible to grade disrespect for God, then this would be the worst form of it. This does not mean that if you are challenged with standing or suffering with an ailment that hampers your ability to stand for long periods that you are to be made to stand during worship; there are always exceptions. But when strong, healthy men and women of God choose to sit during worship, it sends a message of a total disregard for order – especially when these are the same men who will stand for hours to view live sports.

Another offensive practice is the late arrival to service, with some people seeing nothing wrong with walking straight up to the front to secure their usual vantage seats or go onto the pulpit. What do you think this says about you, your church, your pastor, or God? It is about having and setting a standard, representing God, and understanding that you are on holy ground and in His presence and that a show of respect and order will be reflective of who He is. There are times when punctuality may be a challenge, but there are some members who are habitual punctuality offenders and see nothing wrong with having God wait on them to get the programme started. This practice is even more offensive when these are the members charged with the responsibility of conducting the service, whether in the praise and worship team or otherwise. As believers, we are instructed to 'Let all things be done decently and in order' (1 Corinthians 14:40 KJV). There are churches where if you come one minute after the start of the service, you are barred from approaching the altar to lead the congregation in praise and worship. It does not matter if it is the drummer, guitarist, or any other musician; service is conducted without that instrument on that Saturday or Sunday, because it is about recognising the value of order and having respect for the presence of God in our midst. These particular churches model order and, by extension, God.

While there must be order in the conduct of the service, this must not be an excuse to stymie the operation of the Holy Spirit. In fact, allowing the Holy Spirit to take charge during the service is a signal of order, because it is His holy house. Order in a service occurs where the Holy Spirit is in full operation, where the gifts of the Spirit are not usurping each other in their manifestation, where the congregation has a healthy respect for God which manifests in the members' behaviour, where there is full participation and reverence for the presence of God, and where the sanctuary presents as a place where God's people are gathered worshipping, sharing, and having everything in common. Paul addressed order in the service in terms of how congregants are to flow in the Spirit, with believers being commanded to maintain order in the operation and manifestation of the gifts of the Holy Spirit. (See 1 Corinthians 14 KJV.) A service where there is order works for the edification of man and glorification of God.

WALKING ORDERLY

We are called to walk orderly before God, which implies that we are to walk with modesty, proper decorum, and as exemplars of the Word:

> Now we command you, brethren, in the name of our Lord Jesus Christ, that ye withdraw yourselves from every brother that walketh disorderly, and not after the tradition which he received of us. For yourselves know how ye ought to follow us: for we behaved not ourselves disorderly among you; Neither did we eat any man's bread for nought; but wrought with labour and travail night and day, that we might not be chargeable to any of you: Not because we have not power, but to make ourselves an ensample unto you to follow us. ... For we hear that there are some which walk among you disorderly,

working not at all, but are busybodies. (2 Thessalonians 3:6–9, 11 KJV)

Walking orderly is about more than just exhibiting proper decorum; it is about imaging order on earth. God is order; you are created in His image, which means you are a blueprint of order. So your Christian walk should image God on earth. Believers are instructed to: 'Lie not one to another, seeing that ye have put off the old man with his deeds; And have put on the new man, which is renewed in knowledge after the image of him that created him' (Colossians 3:9–10 KJV). The Greek word 'kosmios' for 'orderly' speaks to a Christian's walk needing to be decent, modest, blemish free, blameless, and exemplary.[8] (See 1 Timothy 3:2 KJV.) This is also the sense in which it is used in Acts 21:24 KJV, where we are called upon to walk orderly: '...but that thou thyself also walkest orderly, and keepest the law.' The Hebrew word 'halak' means 'to go, walk, behave', which speaks of one's behaviour, or the way one 'walks in life'. It refers to a believer's walk being required to be upright and righteous. (See Isaiah 33:15 KJV and Micah 2:7 KJV.) It covers walking in righteousness (Proverbs 2:7 KJV), in humility (Micah 6:8 KJV), and in integrity (Psalm 15:2 KJV). We are encouraged to walk blamelessly before God: 'For the LORD God is a sun and shield: the LORD will give grace and glory: no good thing will he withhold from them that walk uprightly' (Psalm 84:11 KJV).

Walking orderly is a multi-tiered concept that refers to the believers' representative responsibility, which means that you are to represent or present God through keeping His law and in your behaviour, conduct, appearance, communication, and relationships. The Bible is awash with examples of how believers are to walk orderly in His presence in their attire, communication, and relationships, all of which are examined below.

IN HIS PRESENCE

At its most basic level of interpretation, walking orderly is about inhabiting and living in His presence, much like Adam did. Most believers understand that when they become blood-washed, they are restored to right relationship with God and given unhindered and free access to His throne. 'Let us therefore come boldly unto the throne of grace that we may obtain mercy, and find grace to help in time of need' (Hebrews 4:16 KJV). Through grace, we are restored to inhabiting His presence, where His fullness dwells. But do we really comprehend what inhabiting His presence entails? Well, this means that daily we are to walk before Him, with Him, and under His cover. 'In His presence' means walking in holiness, uprightness, humility, love, and order – a simple feat if we allow the Holy Spirit to guide and control our lives. It is a call to holiness. 'For I am the LORD your God: ye shall therefore sanctify yourselves, and ye shall be holy; for I am holy' (Leviticus 11:44–45 KJV). Being in His presence means for example peace, healing, wholeness, rightness, power, love, grace, forgiveness, holiness, and mercy.

The presence of God is a place of purity, holiness, judgment and love – a place that is order. Sin cannot inhabit or stand in His presence. Disorder cannot exist in His presence. Man in his fallen state cannot stand in the presence of God, so it is only through the blood of Jesus Christ that we have access to and can dwell in His presence. We are not required to do anything or take any step to live in His presence; we are designated holy, righteous, sanctified, and justified by the blood of Jesus Christ, and so we are fit to inhabit His presence. It is an act of grace that ushers us freely into His presence and allows us to stand.

An example of what happens when man comes into the space or circle of the presence of God is Moses, and the experience is equivalent to walking into the blinding light of holiness. The effect of this was that Moses' skin on his face was left shining with the glory of the aftermath of God's presence, which instilled fear in Aaron and the children of Israel to even approach him. (See Exodus 33:18–23; 34:29 KJV.) Likewise, when the presence of God is in a place, man falls prostrate on his face and the place is infused with the light of His holiness.

The presence of God is a place of power, so if sin presents or disorder infiltrates, there is an instantaneous reinstatement of order. Sometimes this is achieved with an order for execution or a swift reprimand and call to return to order, as occurred many times in the Bible. (See Acts 5:1–12 KJV.) If diseases show up, God's presence is sufficient to cause men, even if struck down at birth, to leave their beds of affliction and come leaping, strutting, and praising into the temple of God. This was demonstrated with the crippled at birth at the gate of the temple called Beautiful. (See Acts 3:2–11 KJV.) If we accept that salvation gives us the key to access His presence, then we must understand the full import of inhabiting God's presence. It is why we are called to walk orderly, and it is why this involves walking in His presence. Yet we constantly fall short of this mark. The Bible makes it clear that walking orderly means walking uprightly, walking in His presence, in the sense of living responsibly, faithfully, and clean before Him. (See Genesis 5:22 NIV.) It is not an optional requirement for a Christian's walk; it is mandatory.

SPIRITUAL ATTIRE

Walking orderly also refers to putting on the proper spiritual attire. The body of Christ has swung from one end of the pendulum to the other in terms of its spiritual attire, or how it presents to the world. The believer's spiritual attire is the outer and inner clothing or cover he wears, and it is an attire of order. One just has to go back to the early Christian church in Acts to see how orderly members walked and the power and order they operated in and presented to the world. That early Christian church operated in purity and oneness before God, having all things in common. (See Acts 4:32 KJV.) The early church was walking orderly in its spiritual dress of order, and so it presented as having a closeness of bond; there was unity, sharing, fellowship, love, holiness, peace, purity, power, and order. So when disorder stepped into the church in the form of Ananias and his wife, Sapphira, it was immediately halted with a death sentence. (See Acts 5:1–11 KJV.)

The modern Christian church is at the opposite extreme of the pendulum, where disorder does not face a death order but is actively operating and alive within the church, and manifesting through the disorderly walk of believers. Walking orderly implies that our conduct must be exemplary as Christians and that our appearances, both physical and spiritual, must be proper. The behaviour and conduct of a believer must model order. The Holy Spirit is our guide as to what is or is not orderly behaviour.

COMMUNICATING CHRIST

Walking orderly is about how we communicate Christ. Once we accept that we inhabit His presence, walking orderly encapsulates how we communicate with and about each other, and what we communicate to those external to our congregation. 'Walk in wisdom toward outsiders, making the best use of the time. Let your speech always be gracious, seasoned with salt, so that you may know how you ought to answer each person' (Colossians 4:5–6 ESV). Can you picture being in the presence of God and having vile conversations or speaking ill of a Christian brother? Or do we step out of His presence when we conduct ourselves in that manner? The Bible tells us: 'But now ye also put off all these; anger, wrath, malice, blasphemy, filthy communication out of your mouth' (Colossians 3:8 KJV). We are clearly to avoid unholy conversations and aim for a clean and holy way of speaking. 'As obedient children, not fashioning yourselves according to the former lust in your ignorance: But as he which hath called you is holy, so be ye holy in all manner of conversation; Because it is written, Be ye holy; for I am holy' (1 Peter 1:14–16 KJV). Here we refer to oral communication, but communication takes various forms. Whatever the form, it is clear that our communication should be pure and becoming of the label of Christianity. Yet it is sometimes difficult to distinguish between the communication of the believer and unbeliever. It is incredible how skilled we have become in passing the buck and in seeing the mote in the eyes of others and not our own. But restoring order mandates that we look first at ourselves and see our defects before we even attempt to point to the flaws in others.

We are required also to communicate the truth of Christ and not heresy; in essence, we are to be doctrinally sound in our teaching of Christ. This is captured in the Bible: 'For there are many unruly and vain talkers and deceivers, specially they of the circumcision: Whose mouths must be stopped, who subvert whole houses, teaching things which they ought not, for filthy lucre's sake' (Titus 1:10 KJV). Filthy communication in the mouths of believers, the preaching of heresy, and error are not unique to the church in Colossae, and we are called to guard against falling for this. We are called as believers to communicate Christ, the sole mediator between God and man and the one in whom all the fullness of the godhead dwells. Clearly, our manner and content of communication are pivotal to walking orderly before God.

ORDER IN RELATIONSHIPS

Another crucial area of walking orderly has to do with our relationships both within and outside the church. It is about our relationship with God, our family members, other believers, and the unsaved man. It is about having God at the centre of our relationships with others to realise order in them. It is about developing, running after, forging, and nurturing Christ-centred relationships. We are enjoined in our relationships with other believers to walk in unity, humility, tolerance, longsuffering and peace. (See Ephesians 4:1–3 KJV.) Christians are instructed to have healthy relationships with family members, friends, and colleagues. The believers' standards for walking orderly in relationships are set out in scripture: believers are to love their neighbours as themselves (see Matthew 22:39 KJV); husbands are to love their wives, and wives must submit to their husbands (see Ephesians 5:22–33 KJV); children are to obey their parents (see Ephesians 6:1–3 KJV); fathers are not to provoke their children to anger (see Ephesians 6:4 KJV), and workers are to obey their bosses and be sure to give Caesar what is his and God what is God's (see Mark 12:17; Ephesians 6:5–7 KJV). These are well-rehearsed and familiar scriptures to every Christian.

Likewise, forming relationships with false gods and intermixing believers with unbelievers are condemned. (See 1 John 5:21 KJV.) Inappropriate relationships within the church are also heavily condemned. (See Ephesians 5:3–12 KJV.) Yet in direct contravention of the call on the believers' lives to image order is the promulgation of inappropriate relationships in the house of God.

This aberration in a Christian's walk is more than just the flesh warring against the spirit man (though it is a cause), and it is more than just disorder operating in and controlling the church. It is about man's choice to walk in disorderly relationships, man's refusal to deny self (not an inability to do so), man ceding of his authority over flesh to disorder, and man's failure to understand and accept that God is order and that imaging order means having orderly relationships. It cannot be any other way, for disorder can never control order; it can manifest but is always dispelled by order. Isn't darkness always dispelled by light? Disorder has no control over the God who is order. Because of this, our relationships can and must reflect order; they must image God.

Finally, God desires that His church be order-centric and not unruly. The order-centric church is one that is fully clothed with the presence of God and demonstrates that it is walking orderly by communicating Christ to its internal and external patrons and where its leadership and other congregants are imaging the God who is order. Order is the core for the end-time agenda of God to be fulfilled. It is why we are called to order by a God who is order.

CHAPTER 4

THE WAR AGAINST DIVINE ORDER

Before the creation of the world, there was a war launched against divine order, and this continues up to the present time. Divine order refers to the nature and character of God, which is heavenly, holy, just, and pure, as well as how He acts or operates to bring about or fulfil His purposes on earth. God is divine order; it is who He is, and it is what He does (i.e., pronounces/proclaims) or how He acts (i.e., arranging events to achieve order). To simplify this further, it can be stated that there are two distinct facets to this concept of divine order; the first is internal (who He is), and the second, external (how He acts).

Throughout the writing of this book, this fundamental truth that God is order has been the bedrock principle, and it is not an unconvincing case to make that God is divine order, given that His nature is supreme holiness. By virtue of His divinity, it means that as order, He is intrinsically and inherently holy and divine or set apart. It is part of His nature and divinity to be order and to present as the antithesis of disorder. It is not the intention here to make a case for this foundational truth that God is divine order and that divine order is God, for these are indivisible concepts. The focus of this chapter rather is on how God externalises as divine order in the war against Him. Since God is divine order, it begs the question, then, how are Christians able to navigate in the natural realm to image a God who is divine order? What is the outlet or bridge in place to allow the seamless flow of order from God to the believer?

THE EXTERNALISATION OF DIVINE ORDER

Externalising divine order from who He is innately means that it is proceeding directly from God. When externalised, it means simply that divine order is God, orchestrated and executed through the believer's life. In other words, it is a heavenly agenda being accomplished through an earthly manifestation. If perchance you are still asking, 'So then what, really, is divine order?', I will take you back to the Greek word '*diatássō*', which means 'to arrange or to set things in order' but also 'to command with detailed instructions'. In other words, it means 'to issue a command with *full* authority' because it takes into account all that is necessary to *lay down a proper order.*[9] In essence, it is divine order (command) proceeding from God (divine deity) to man, arranging and setting things in order.

In my search for even greater clarity on this issue, I turned to God, who dropped this definition in my Spirit while I was seeking answers from Him on exactly this question: 'Divine order is the sequence of events crafted by God to bring glory to His name. It has nothing to do with man's input but has everything to do with his obedience.' This definition is loaded, so it needs to be marinated upon before proceeding further. Why does God describe Himself as 'the sequence of events' He has fashioned for His purpose? Is God saying that His divine order is meant to be realised, no matter the choices made by man? Or is God saying that He operates by creating and arranging (sequencing) actions that will lead ultimately to His name being glorified? Or can it be that He is saying here that by virtue of being divine order, He is crafting or creating situations and circumstances in the earth in the life of man that will all lead to the glory of His name? In other words, did divine order always have a plan to counteract man's disobedience and disorder, and to arrange it to restore order and bring glory to His name? This means that even man's disobedience (whether in the garden of Eden or now) is being arranged for God's glory. It is about God strategically orchestrating events or creating an arrangement of actions that will lead right back to, and bring glory to, His name. Yes, that was the rhema word revealing new insight into God as divine order.

When God dropped this definition in my spirit, I did not understand its full import until I began to analyse it and seriously mull over it. The expression 'sequence of events' refers to and is linked directly to the Greek words for order – 'diatássō', 'taxis', 'tagma', and 'epidiorthoo' – as it speaks to arranging, an arrangement, structure, order, succession, and taking action to put in order. Instantly I knew that the ultimate example of this divine order in operation was Jesus Christ. But I felt compelled by the Holy Spirit to search for other examples of God operating to sequence events in the Bible to lead right back to bringing glory to His name, and almost immediately, the name Jonah was dropped in my spirit. The story of Jonah is analysed in depth below, but first, to understand divine order as being externalised or issuing from God, it is necessary to look at the concepts of obedience and disobedience.

OBEDIENCE VERSUS DISOBEDIENCE

There must be a reason for God directing us to look at divine order through the prism of obedience and disobedience. When light comes through a prism, it refracts (breaks up) and bends to present its various forms and colours. Likewise, in discussing divine order, through the use of these two constructs as a prism for breaking the concept up, it is clear that obedience causes order and disobedience causes disorder. An example of divine order externalised as obedience is Christ, who came to execute or manifest God's command to set things in order by overthrowing disorder. Jesus Christ is thus the ultimate symbol of obedience to divine order. His obedience was manifested first by His giving up of His throne and deity to take on the form of man. Then there was His obedience to dying on the cross, whereby He displayed humility to gain the victory over disorder. 'And being found in human form, he humbled himself by becoming obedient to the point of death, even death on a cross' (Philippians 2:8 ESV). This is the example that believers are to image. Jesus understood that God's divine order requires obedience even unto death. Jesus Christ is the epitome of divine order, since He is the Word of God. When God speaks, He speaks only order. (See John 1:1 KJV.)

Another example where obedience was maintained even unto death or intended execution is the story of Shadrach, Meshach, and Abednego. This example is an illustration of obedience leading to deliverance by means of these three Hebrew boys exhibiting absolute faith and trust in God to turn up and deliver them from death by the fiery furnace. In the face of a decree by King Nebuchadnezzar to fall down and worship the golden image set up by him or face death by fire, Shadrach, Meshach, and Abednego stood resolute. 'If it be so, our God whom we serve is able to deliver us from the burning fiery furnace, and he will deliver us out of thine hand, O king. But if not, be it known unto thee, O king, that we will not serve thy gods, nor worship the golden image which thou hast set up' (Daniel 3:17–18 KJV).

In response to their outspoken faith and demonstrable obedience to their God not to worship any other God but Him, King Nebuchadnezzar commanded that the furnace be heated seven times hotter than normal and that they be bound and flung inside, fully clothed. This act led to the fire devouring the men who threw Shadrach, Meshach, and Abednego into the furnace. However, the Hebrew boys were left untouched by the fire. God, who was orchestrating the sequence of events to bring glory to His name through obedience, turned up as divine order. '… Lo, I see four men loose, walking in the midst of the fire, and they have no hurt; and the form of the fourth is like the Son of God' (Daniel 3: 25 KJV). What is even more telling is that this searing hot fire had no power to singe their hair, torch their clothes, or leave the pungent smell of fire and smoke on them.

This story of the three Hebrew boys is a powerful staging of divine order in operation, and it goes to show how obedience, faith, and trust can be used as ducts for the glory of God. It is a clear exhibition of how God acts through a sequence of events that He crafted (for Nebuchadnezzar's decree was the tool used by God) to bring glory to His name. It had nothing to do with man's input and everything to do with his obedience. In like manner, our obedience to God can cause Him to deliver us from the fiery trials we find ourselves in; even if we find ourselves bound and cast into a fire to perish, we must recognise the sequence of events being divinely orchestrated and exercise obedience to bring glory to our God. How many of us can say, as these three Hebrew boys did, that we have faith that God will deliver us, although regardless of that, we will be obedient to the Word of God even unto death? Jesus did exactly this; He remained humble and obedient even unto the death of the cross.

Divine order is also seen through the disobedience of man, in which case God sequences the events and – again without the input of man, except his obedience – glory is brought to the name of God. It is to be made clear that disobedience is the mirror image of disorder and is one of the spirits through which the devil operates in man. But disobedience is unable to prevail against God. You may ask why and point to what is manifesting in the world and in the affairs of man, and to the seeming triumph of disorder over order. Remember the definition given by God for divine order? Well, it is precisely because divine order means that God is operating to sequence events to bring glory to His name, without man's input, that disobedience is trumped by order. God even uses man's disobedience to bring glory to His name, and no, this is not a contradiction – it is truth. The Bible is overflowing with examples where His divine order was manifested despite disobedience. The difference or qualification is that divine order here introduces the element of grace, which through obedience leads to man turning from his disobedience to obedience and the glory going to God's name.

Let us look at an example of disobedience to divine order externalised – Jonah. The sequence of events which took place in Jonah's story was crafted by God to accomplish His spoken word. In externalising as divine order, God's will is implemented even though Jonah was disobedient. God gave an order to Jonah to preach judgment on the city of Nineveh: 'Go to Nineveh, that great city, and proclaim [judgment] against it, for their wickedness has come up before Me' (Jonah 1:2 AMP). In response to this divine order externalised, Jonah decides to disobey God and to create his own sequence of events, which was self-made disorder. Jonah acted by trying to put distance between divine order and himself by escaping to the most remote of the Phoenician trading cities, Tarshish, only to find out he could not run away from the presence of the Lord and his duty as God's prophet. (See Jonah 1:3 AMP.)

Disobedience is one vehicle used by the devil to cause man to yield to his sinful human nature and try to sabotage God's order. We clearly see, however, that God's divine order has consequences when obeyed or disobeyed. In the case of Jonah, disobedience unleashed a violent storm. 'But the LORD hurled a great wind toward the sea, and there was a violent tempest on the sea so that the ship was about to break up' (Jonah 1:4 AMP). Jonah's disobedience then spilled over to impact and threaten the lives of those connected to him through his sin. This points to how a decision of someone to walk in disobedience, who is not even closely connected to you, can bring chaos into your life and the lives of those around the disobedient person. What is created here is clearly 'disorder by association'. But do not forget that divine order means that God is sequencing the events. He is in control; He is never taken by surprise, because He is using this to bring glory to His name. Interestingly enough, Jonah is asleep in the midst of the havoc created by his disobedience. There are many 'shipwreck makers' who go around wreaking havoc through their disobedience and causing it to spill over and impact the lives of many, while they sleep through the storm or seem to be immune from the detrimental impact of their actions. You may wish to ask, whom have I interacted with that has caused disorder in my life? It brings us right back to the need to guard against disorder in our lives. Sometimes shipwreck makers can sleep comfortably and uninterrupted through the utter mayhem brought on by their disobedience, as Jonah did; but do not allow this to devastate your life. Watch and be on guard.

Let us continue to examine Jonah as the tempest is raging. At this point, God is introduced as the creator of the 'sea', where the disorder is taking place, and of the 'dry land', where order will be executed. This was disclosed upon Jonah admitting to being responsible for the disorder and his confession as to his belief system. 'So he said to them, "I am a Hebrew, and I [reverently] fear and worship the LORD, the God of heaven, who made the sea and the dry land"' (Jonah 1:9 AMP). Jonah did not deny his God, even in the midst of his storm. His reaction should be the response of all believers in God when faced with a tempest. It should be a declaration of who we are in Jesus Christ. Our words should be a testament of our God in the situations we face. When Jonah spoke of God, he revealed who God was in that situation. It did not prevent him from being flung overboard and into the midst of the violent, raging sea. This state of affairs was being divinely ordered, as the God who is divine order was orchestrating and coordinating the events. Remember: one of the definitions of 'divine order' is 'God-inspired command with detailed instruction', so we ought not be surprised or astonished when there is a continuum of God-orchestrated events in play. God even arranged a great fish to preserve His order. 'Now the LORD had prepared (appointed, destined) a great fish to swallow Jonah. And Jonah was in the stomach of the fish three days and three nights' (Jonah 1:17 AMP). The symbolism here is not lost, for Jonah is a type of Christ except that Jesus' sojourn in the grave was a result of obedience – not disobedience, as with Jonah. Divine order was operational in both cases, to bring glory to God's name. The Bible says that God watches over His word (order) until it is manifested or is performed. (See Jeremiah 1:12 AMP.) This showcases God's confidence and persistence in having His 'divine order' fulfilled.

As the story progresses, we see that Jonah's disobedience has brought disorder in his life and the lives of others. However, he did not just stay there; he repented, causing God to have him expectorated from the belly of the fish. God, who has crafted this sequence of events, is willing to forgive Jonah of his sin and to cleanse him from all unrighteousness, disobedience, and disorder, in which he wilfully found himself. This is how God operates with all believers in Jesus Christ. It took the repentance of Jonah to get reprieve from the situation. Then God mandated that obedience be displayed. 'Now the word of the LORD came to Jonah the second time, saying, "Go to Nineveh the great city and declare to it the message which I am going to tell you"' (Jonah 3:1–2 AMP). Once Jonah has embraced God's divine order and is dutifully executing the plan of God for his life, he is walking in order. This even brought exculpation to the sinners who ordinarily would have attracted the judgment of God. (See Jonah 3:9–10 AMP.) Jonah's obedience to God's divine order, through his repentance, won the salvation of a nation and brought glory to God's name. Even the king of Nineveh declared a fast throughout the land for every human and all animals. Jonah's story shows how God's divine order operates in our lives to bring glory to His name. God's divine order has a built-in measure of grace; you do not get what you deserve because of His love for you.

Divine order externalised is, therefore, the spoken Word of God manifested in the earth. Whatever He declares will come to pass, even though it may seem that man's disobedience can deter the outcome; this is so because He is the Alpha and Omega, the beginning and the ending. He knows the outcome simultaneously with the beginning; nothing surprises God. But God gives man an opportunity to repent when he has disobeyed or rebelled against His Word. When God issues judgment on a nation, people, or individual, there is always an opportunity that goes with it for genuine repentance. A repentant heart God will not despise, since it leads to salvation. (See 2 Corinthians 7:9–10 KJV.)

Let us look briefly at the contrast between how divine order operated in the case of Nineveh and in the cases of Sodom and Gomorrah. All three cities were destined to be destroyed, however, one was saved and the other two were destroyed. What was different was simply the existence of genuine repentance on the part of one city against a conscious decision to continue participating in rebellion and disorder. Using these cases as a backdrop to divine order as a sequence of events crafted to bring glory to God's name, we are peering into a looking glass and seeing the intricate details of salvation in action for a lost world. Both Jonah and Abraham reasoned with God, and we see the compassion and love of God emerge to bring salvation in one instance; and on the other hand, we see God moving to execute judgment. Do you think Sodom and Gomorrah would have been destroyed if Abraham had found some repentant souls therein? (See Genesis 18:32 KJV.) The Bible states that even Lot was complacent and did not take the warning from the angels with haste. (See Genesis 19:16 KJV.) He was actually 'grabbed' by the hand and hurried out of the city. We know that his wife disobeyed the instructions of the angels not to look back and met her death by being turned into a pillar of salt. Sin is sin, and we need to understand that it breeds disorder, which is the polar opposite of divine order. Disorder, disobedience, rebellion, and unrepentant hearts cannot prevail against a God who is divine order. Disorder stems from direct disobedience of God's instruction or command. But be assured that the God who is order can impact your disorderly life to set it in order, but you must be prepared to repent and walk in obedience. The very fact that God is order indicates that we are to image this order, as we are created in the image and likeness of our Father. You may walk in disobedience or forfeit your participation as a useful vessel of God, but

His divine order will be executed in His time for His glory, with or without you. At the end of the day, God's divine order mandates obedience, even if it requires a turning away from disobedience or disorder.

THE POWER OF PRAYER

If divine order is God creating, sequencing, or arranging events to bring glory to His name and man has no input in this except to exercise obedience, then as believers in Jesus Christ, we must acquire this obedience through prayer. Prayer is like intravenous therapy which gives the life-sustaining water to Christians. It is the blueprint to living a powerful, consistent, and obedient life. Hence, prayer and obedience make a formidable partnership for executing God's divine order. Continually walking in obedience can be realised only through prayer, as it is the medium through which the believer communicates with God and allows himself to be helped by the Holy Spirit. So, as believers in Jesus Christ, we acquire obedience through a powerful prayer life. This is what God is calling believers to when He invites us to be sensitised, equipped, and trained in the art of becoming orders experts.

Prayer is yet another avenue through which divine order is externalised, for we cannot begin to fathom imaging the God who is order without prayer. Prayer single-handedly connects and reconnects us to the very source of life – God the Father, the Son, and the Holy Spirit. There are many examples of this truth in the Bible. When the Word of God was made flesh and lived among us, His lifeline to His heavenly home, while in this earthly realm, was prayer. The Bible has recorded countless occasions when Jesus Christ escaped the crowds and retreated to a solitary place just to pray. 'And in the morning, rising up a great while before day, he went out, and departed into a solitary place, and there prayed' (Mark 1:35 KJV; Luke 5:16 KJV). Jesus Christ understood that His permanent connection to His source of life and existence was prayer – deep, meaningful prayer. When you, as a child of God, heir to the kingdom of God, understand the impact you can have on the earth, your prayer life changes. You will seek to engage in strategic warfare and to fine-tune your conversations with God. It becomes less of you and more of impacting the earth. Your prayer life is crucial in that it impacts the way you walk, talk, and act on a daily basis. Prayer is the 'wear' used to image God. It is, therefore, imperative to understand that an integral part of God as divine order requires a Christian to live in prayer. This is essentially what this book is about; it is about honing your warfare praying skills to have a greater impact on the kingdom of darkness.

We need to understand that the prayer act is not confined to a time, a posture, a manner of speaking, the rehashing of fixed words, or a weekly meeting but is who we are as believers, engaged in conversation with our Father. And such conversations may run the gamut from casual, calm, thankful, and recognising and lifting up the name of God to being authoritative, commanding, or powerfully and forcefully impacting the kingdom of darkness. As believers, when we engage in prayer, we should ensure that our skills are continually being sharpened by increasing our knowledge about how we are to pray. This is where obedience will assist in pushing us ahead, for as we submit to learning how to enhance our warfare skills, we will become more effective prayer warriors.

Prayer is communion with God; it is the pipeline through which a believer is fed or connected to his source. It is our means of tapping into and inhaling the majesty of God; it is our lifeline to Our Heavenly Father. Through prayer, we receive satisfaction of our needs, but prayer is not meant only to be a way of soliciting satisfaction of our wants and needs. In fact, when we seek, through prayer, to be used as channels for God's kingdom to be manifested on earth, our needs are actually taken care of without us even having to pray about them. This type of selfless praying is so powerful that it is capable of shaking the kingdom of darkness, circumventing and warding off the attacks of the devil, and whipping disorder into order. It is the type of prayer engaged in by true intercessors – externalised and selfless seeking of God for others, our leaders, the nation, the world, and

God's kingdom to be manifested on the earth. The God who is order is calling His children to refocus their prayer lives from self and using prayer to beg for the fulfilment of needs (God knows our needs) towards bombarding the kingdom of darkness with strategic, targeted, and powerful prayer. He is calling believers to understand the arsenal of weapons in their prayer kit and use them properly and in a targeted manner to destroy the enemy. '(For after all these things do the Gentiles seek:) for your heavenly Father knoweth that ye have need of all these things. But seek ye first the kingdom of God, and his righteousness; and all these things shall be added unto you. Take therefore no thought for the morrow: for the morrow shall take thought for the things of itself. Sufficient unto the day is the evil thereof' (Matthew 6:32–34 KJV).

Prayer requires a believer to be an acute listener. The Bible extols the virtues of listening: 'Why spend money on what is not bread, and your labor on what does not satisfy? Listen, listen to me, and eat what is good, and you will delight in the richest of fare. Give ear and come to me; listen, that you may live' (Isaiah 55:2–3 NIV). Prayer means actively listening to the voice of God to enact the will of God. Without prayer, how can you truly know what God requires from and for you? Prayer translates into who we are and not what we do. Hence the call to become an orders expert – one who is engaged in the active listening to the voice of the Holy Spirit, one with increased perception and discernment, and one with the humility to allow the will of God to be enacted through one's life. The war against divine order, which is how God operates or sequences events to realise His purposes on earth, is a war designed to put a divide between man and God. Prayer bridges this chasm; as believers engage in communal interaction with God, it closes the gap and promotes the will of God on earth. Prayer is our only way to communicate with God in this earthly realm. A powerful prayer life makes you an unstoppable force against the kingdom of darkness. You cannot become an orders expert without developing a strong prayer life.

CHAPTER 5

TYPES OF ORDERS (1)

A Christian has the ability, in prayer, to make and issue various types of orders to deal with the numerous situations in his life. In fact, when you pray, you make orders without even realising that you are doing so. This means that every Christian is involved in the business of seeking and making spiritual orders, whether he recognises it or not and even if some are more adept at it than others. If you have the qualification but are untrained, ill-equipped or lacking the skills, you may not be as effective an intercessor or prayer warrior as you can be. As with anything, training brings insight, growth, understanding, and skills which can make you a more effective prayer warrior. Understanding also that no one order is suitable for every situation will make you into a more effective prayer advocate or intercessor. So when you are making spiritual orders in prayer to deal with problems for which the specific orders may not be available, required, or capable of eliminating the problem, you are in effect praying ineffective prayers. It is no wonder why a Christian may find himself praying for years about a particular problem or need without getting answers. It is not always a case where the answer is delayed or not granted; it may simply be a matter of you not having prayed for the right order, meaning it will never be granted. Sometimes you pray for the same order that was granted in another person's situation, but it may not be appropriate to solve your problem. Check what you have been praying for and not getting a response to; see if a different approach or application for a different order might bring results, and check whether you have the right to seek that order of God. It is very much like praying amiss. If you are applying for an order that is not available in your situation, then, you cannot get it. James 4:3 KJV says, 'Ye ask, and receive not, because ye ask amiss, that ye may consume it upon your lusts.' If you apply for an order that will not be the right fix or the request comes from a place of selfishness or a desire to satisfy self, you may be denied it. So the reason or basis for your request will determine whether or not you are granted it. Sometimes you may need more than one order or to vary an order to make it suit your circumstances, or a different order entirely to what would have fixed a similar problem. If you are in need of having something released or exposed, then you cannot be praying for a committal order; what you need in that situation is to pray specifically for a habeas corpus order or a release order, whichever one is the balm for the sore.

GROUNDS

Every order sought in the earthly court must be based on valid legal grounds that will be recognised by a court of law, and it is the same way with the heavenly court. Do not be fooled into believing otherwise; it is time for Christians to start understanding, operating on, and applying kingdom principles correctly, including principles relevant to guiding your approach and behaviour before the heavenly court. A 'ground' refers to the cause or reason or basis for bringing your application or request before God, which must be valid and not contrived or made up. For instance, you do not just pray or seek an injunctive, restraining, or dismissal order without having a basis or ground for so doing. Now, do not get me wrong, you can glorify God anytime and anywhere, you can engage in a prayer of thanksgiving at any point, you can pray soft prayers to maintain communication with God at any time, and you can praise and worship at will, but there are certain types of prayerful engagements for which there must be grounds. You do not jump willy-nilly or haphazardly into spiritual warfare without a cause. Prayers of thanksgiving do not require the use of strategic warfare devices, but when you want to seek a specific order of

God, you must have spiritual grounds or a cause. By this I mean that you must have sustained a wrong (spiritual attack) that provides the ground for you to approach and request an order, whether that order be dismissive, injunctive, restraining, or otherwise. Believers usually have grounds when we come before God to do battle, but we do not even think of them like that. But now God wants us to put ourselves in the knowing of what we are doing; this helps to sharpen our warfare skills.

There are certain instances when we enter into warfare and have no grounds, so we find ourselves uttering ineffective, thoughtless, and unwise orders in our prayers. Let me try to be clearer by giving an example: if you desire a thing to consume it upon your own selfish lust or you believe you are being denied it unjustifiably by a person or situation but you are really in error, and you engage under these false pretences in spiritual warfare and issue orders, you may be praying without grounds. You have no cause for bringing that suit or application before God, so it will not be granted. The Bible refers to 'praying amiss', which is the biblical concept of praying without grounds – it refers to a baseless, unfounded ground or a non-existent cause for approaching the throne in prayer. In the earthly court, if you have no cause of action that is the ground for filing the claim, your case will be thrown out. It is the same in the heavenly court, but there it is called 'praying amiss'. So it is important to determine whether you are praying amiss. You do not question whether you are praying amiss, because it is easier to operate in denial and blame God for not listening or failing to grant your requests. Some of you may not blame God overtly but may put the non-response to your prayer on yourself, saying it is something you are not doing, while others love to gloss over God's silence with the holy plasters of 'It is not my time yet' or 'It is not your will, God.' Well, it will not be your time now or ever if you are praying amiss, and it will serve you better if you accept that self must be checked and searched feverishly and painstakingly to uncover whether, in fact, your prayer is being made amiss.

The word 'amiss' refers to an erroneous, inappropriate, incorrect, awry, mistaken, or wrong basis for doing something. In essence, it refers to acting without a cause or ground to so do. In this case, it is for praying or engaging in spiritual warfare. Yes, even you can pray amiss; this is not a concept reserved for those who do not know Jesus Christ the way you do. God is speaking directly to you, so don't put up your hand to ward off what is being said here. It is a word for you. Understand this: when we pray amiss, it is tantamount to bringing an application without a proper basis or ground and asking God to fix it or to ignore that you have no cause for bringing that case before Him, because, after all, He should be grateful that you gave your life to Him. It does not work so, and it is time we start taking the responsibility to ensure that when we place our matters before Him, we are not denied our requests because we have no grounds for bringing them, because our grounds are skewed wrongly by our lusts, or because we simply have no bases to bring those types of applications. It is time to stop praying amiss.

IDENTIFYING THE RIGHT ORDER

Apart from how you bring the application before the heavenly court, you must know beforehand what order you want to seek or have issued in a matter. You must also know what order is available to solve your problem. This involves pressing into the Holy Spirit and allowing Him to lead, guide, influence, and assist you with how to pray. This applies even to the best prayer intercessor, because it is more than just the words you utter; it is about those words being spirit injected, spirit inspired, spirit guided, and precise so the right order is issued every time. The Bible states: 'Likewise the Spirit also helpeth our infirmities: for we know not what we should pray for as we ought: but the Spirit itself maketh intercession for us with groanings which cannot be uttered' (Romans 8:26 KJV). Within this verse is the recognition that the Spirit is operating inside us to help and empower us to intercede accurately and as spiritual sharpshooters when we issue our orders. That is how I read it, so I accept that any helplessness I may feel or any struggle for words should be ceded to the Holy Spirit, whose role is to intercede on my behalf and assist me when I pray or enter the heavenly court to make my application for various spiritual orders. He operates here both as my spiritual advocate (intercessor) and my instructing attorney (i.e., my helper or assistant). (See Romans 8:26 KJV.) The Bible also tells us that Jesus Christ is our advocate and intercessor before the heavenly court: 'And if any man sin, we have an advocate with the Father, Jesus Christ the righteous' (1 John 2:1 KJV). This is stated thus: 'Who is he that condemneth? It is Christ that died, yea rather, that is risen again, who is even at the right hand of God, who also maketh intercession for us' (Romans 8:34 KJV). This reality of Jesus Christ living to make intercession for us and operating as our advocate is also confirmed in the Bible. (See Hebrews 7:25 KJV.) Jesus is also our 'betwixt man' and 'mediator', which points to His role before the heavenly court as the spiritual bridge and intercessor. 'For there is one God, and one mediator between God and men, the man Christ Jesus' (1 Timothy 2:5 KJV). Jesus Christ is presented also as the mediator of the new and better covenant. (See Hebrews 8:6; 9:15; 12:24 KJV.) It is clear that the Holy Spirit will help us with seeking and making the right orders when we pray.

Orders are specific, so we need to know how to pray targeted prayers and how to issue the correct order for the problem to avoid having to return to amend or vary the order obtained. This means that as Christians, we must become adept at identifying, seeking, and making the right orders, as well as praying solution-oriented prayers. It is time for Christians to stop being 'whirlwind prayer warriors' and 'tornado intercessors'; these people are interceding, but everything is spinning chaotically out of control and keeps circling around at them. It is time to calmly and confidently issue the orders to deal with the storms you are caught up in. Then accept by faith that the order, having been issued, is sufficient to dispose of the matter in terms as directed therein. Become an orders expert by learning how to craft, apply for, ensure you are entitled to, and can correctly identify the order appropriate for your problem. This spiritual acumen can be obtained only with the help of the Holy Spirit.

STANDING

Another crucial aspect for making an application for an order is standing, which is different to grounds for the requests but speaks to your entitlement to obtain the order. In other words, you must have some right to it; this speaks to your entitlement to be a party in a matter or one who has an interest in it.[10] So, as a Christian, you have a right to place your claim for relief or help before the heavenly court or defend an attack against you by bringing it before your God. In legal circles, we refer to this as 'standing' (sometimes with the Latin term 'locus standi'). Similarly, in Christian circles, you are required to have 'standing'. Your salvation gives you that right, the standing, the entitlement to approach the throne, and the authority to have an immediate audience. Grace is the key to unlocking or clothing yourself with standing, for it is by grace that we are saved and not in our own self or by our own works. Your personal relationship with Christ Jesus also gives you standing to approach the heavenly court. You must ensure that you have the right or are dressed with the authority to operate from the position of the applicant or respondent in a matter. A man cannot walk off the street and into an earthly court and get an audience; he must be a party to the action or have an interest, such as an intervener, to be given a hearing. He must have standing to be heard.

POSITIONING

It is imperative that you understand your positioning when you pray. This is where many Christians get licks, because they pray without that understanding. Positioning requires you to understand the position or vantage point from which you must pray and how you are to address the heavenly court or your relationship with the court. It is like having a gold card with unlimited funds or power to purchase but choosing to queue up for a loan. Positioning is linked to standing but ups the ante a lot in terms of the authority you wield in praying or accessing the heavenly court. Positioning includes the authority with which you operate, but it is more than just you saying, 'I know I have the authority in Christ Jesus.' Positioning refers to recognising, when you are operating in that authority, that you are doing so from a higher spiritual vantage point; it is like exercising heavenly authority in the spirit realm. It calls upon you to pierce the spiritual veil with the authority that is given to you by Christ Jesus and with the help of His Holy Spirit, and to do your warfare in that realm and at that level.

Positioning means you will have a knowing that, when victories are won in the spirit realm, what manifests in the physical or earthly realm is inconsequential, for you operate and inhabit a sphere that is beyond the comprehension of the physical mind or eyes. Your positioning will allow you to see what is not yet visible, hear what man's ears cannot hear, and know what is, without the revelation of that knowledge being known in the physical realm. It is the same authority that Christ Jesus used to enter into the kingdom of darkness and take the keys from Satan – that is positioning; it is a manner of operating and a place from which you operate that tolerates no resistance. (See Matthew 16:18–19 KJV.) Simply put, positioning means that your place (position) in prayer is heavenly so your prayers must be heavenly prayers and not earthly bound. Positioning is the spiritual plane from which a Christian prays and the authority possessed at that higher level. It is that authority with which a Christian prays or can command the spirit world that is vested in him by Jesus Christ that is unalike anything I have seen – a heavenly authority. It is the authority and power that come with being blood-washed, blood-flushed, Holy Spirit–infused, sanctified, justified, and purified.

Christians speak from a different vantage point or authority because our relationship with Jesus Christ gives us a different access. We have gold card access, which gives us unlimited spiritual power to trample upon and destroy the works of the enemy. We read of our power, claim that we believe we have power, but fail to appropriate and operate in the power. We allow self to tell us that, despite what the Bible says, we cannot do what Jesus Christ did or even greater works than He accomplished. (See John 14:12 KJV.) We allow ourselves to be fooled into accepting that the power and authority the apostles walked in during the times of the book of Acts are not applicable to us. 'And fear came upon every soul: and many wonders and signs were done by the apostles' (Acts 2:43; 5:12 KJV). We say we believe the Word, and even that we have faith, but our actions say otherwise. We are in awe when a miracle occurs among us, as if that were not supposed to be the norm and the level of power in which we are to operate. We become prophesy chasers rather than operating in the prophetic realm as a normalised part of our Christian walk. We submit to and die from myriad diseases rather than use the power in us to speak healing and wholeness. And we allow the enemy to trample on our marriages, our children's lives, and our finances instead of trampling on the enemy and making him hightail it out of our lives. We present as weak, feeble, incapacitated Christians instead of walking, talking, and operating in the positioning (power and authority) in which we are called to function.

Some of us do not even know the word 'positioning' or have interest in finding out about it, because it is safer to not know. If we do not know, then we are not responsible for operating at that lower carnal level and understanding; we are excused. But God wants us to understand our positioning in Him and to come up to that level and authority when we pray. If we continue to refuse to appreciate our positioning in prayer, we will continue spinning in mud, being earthly prayer warriors when we are called to control, invade, pierce, and dominate the spiritual realm or heavens.

The concept of positioning is best explained by applying it to something with which you are familiar. This is typified by the earthly court, where an attorney who is referred to as an 'officer of the court' has rights and privileges to approach, to be heard, and to address the bench that an ordinary man does not have. Even his seat in the court is differently positioned to give him that easier access to the ear of the court. Positioning refers to the place and the vantage point from which you pray (heavenly) and the authority with which you speak. With the heavenly court, you have even greater priority to the throne of God than an attorney before an earthly court. An attorney must satisfy the requirements of the earthly court to get a hearing including being on record for a party in the matter, being on the updated roll of attorneys (by paying the yearly subscription fee) and being appropriately attired. Salvation gives you free access to the throne. (See Hebrews 4:15–16 KJV.) It gives you direct access to the ear of God. 'For the eyes of the Lord are on the righteous and his ears are attentive to their prayer, but the face of the Lord is against those who do evil' (1 Peter 3:12 NIV). This unhindered access to be heard by God or to have Him listen to your prayer is confirmed in several other scriptures (e.g., 2 Kings 13:4; 2 Kings 20:5 NIV, and Deuteronomy 9:19 NIV).

Positioning is different from knowing your position, but the two concepts are linked. Knowing your position refers to the titles or designations ascribed to parties in an action (such as 'claimant' or 'defendant'), as well as your stand on a given issue (such as being in agreement, being in disagreement, conceding, or contesting.) It is critical to know your position before approaching a heavenly court, because you may be seeking or issuing orders from different designations or stances.

For example, a reversal order or a setting-aside order may be needed to ward off an attack that was launched against you, so in that situation you may be operating from a defensive position. You must put yourself in the know as to whether you are entering the battle from an offensive or a defensive stance. Knowing your position then refers to your designation (title) in the matter and stance on an issue, whilst positioning is an operational term; that is, it relates to the point from which you operate to launch your attack (the spiritual realm) and the heavenly authority you employ to decimate your attackers. Positioning means you engage not in earthly battles but in spiritual battles in which you wield spiritual authority over the principalities and powers of the air and against 'the rulers of the darkness of this world, against spiritual wickedness in high places' (Ephesians 6:12 KJV). To put it another way, positioning is using the authority and power He has given you to infiltrate the spiritual realm and operating from that sphere to make orders that impact the earth. It comes from knowing that you have direct access to God and are empowered to operate at that level of spiritual warfare.

BRINGING THE APPLICATION

You are coming before a God who is order with your petition, so your attire must be in order and your form (application) must be acceptable. The Bible says we are to enter His court dressed with praise and thanksgiving and to don the garment of sacrifice; this refers to the attire of our Christian profession. (See Psalm 100:4 KJV). Also encapsulated under this banner of Christian attire would be forgiveness before approaching God in prayer, as outlined in the guidelines for how to pray in the Lord's Prayer. Our Christian dress also includes the putting on of the whole armour of God, as set out in Ephesians 6:10–18 KJV:

> Finally, my brethren, be strong in the Lord, and in the power of His might. Put on the whole armour of God, that ye may be able to stand against the wiles of the devil. For we wrestle not against flesh and blood, but against principalities, against powers, against the rulers of the darkness of this world, against spiritual wickedness in high places. Wherefore take unto you the whole armour of God, that ye may be able to withstand in the evil day, and having done all, to stand. Stand therefore, having your loins girt about with truth, and having on the breastplate of righteousness; And your feet shod with the preparation of the gospel of peace; Above all, taking the shield of faith, wherewith ye shall be able to quench all the fiery darts of the wicked. And take the helmet of salvation, and the sword of the Spirit, which

is the word of God: Praying always with all prayer and supplication in the Spirit, and watching thereunto with all perseverance and supplication for all saints.

With respect to the form of the application, the principles set out above are tools for bringing spiritual suit, so they are very important. First you must have grounds; then the standing. You must then adopt your correct prayer positioning and know your rights and how to make the correct spiritual application. When bringing your application in prayer, you are required to be more than attired properly; you will also need to do the following:

MAKE YOUR APPLICATION CLEAR

Making the correct spiritual application or request requires you to be familiar with the available remedies (orders) and to ensure that the order being sought is appropriate for your situation. Types of spiritual orders are dealt with comprehensively in the next chapter, so I will discuss here only briefly the reasons for needing to know your orders. You need to know, even before you pray, that you are applying for a solution that is an available remedy for your situation. Let me try to explain this in even simpler terms: If you have a land dispute with your neighbour, you should not be praying for a divorce decree to be pronounced against your neighbour. What you may need is an injunctive order against his trespass onto your land, or a declaratory order – not a decree nisi against your neighbour's husband. You cannot get a decree nisi, because you are not married to your neighbour's husband. A decree nisi is an available remedy but it is not an appropriate solution to your problem. Further, the two types of orders (decree nisi and trespass to land) run in different legal streams and are not available in the same jurisdiction. One type of order is available in the civil stream, and the other in the family jurisdiction. A decree nisi causes a provisional cut to the marital relationship but is ineffective to solve a land dispute, so what you get from this prayer is a null-and-void order. Who really wants to be asking for a non-solution to your problem? Yet many of us pray for things that are incapable of solving our problems; we seek void orders and then wonder why God is not answering. He is answering; it is just that what you are seeking is the wrong order to put an end to your problem.

Another example is that of an unemployed man praying for money to come to him. What he needs is an order for the release of a job, which is a better fix than the temporary release of finances. He may be granted that interim order, but it is a temporary fix and his problem remains. How many of us get temporary fixes for our problems based on our prayers and then subsequently realise that the problem still exists? This occurs because we have asked for the wrong order. Yet another example is a retiree praying for a house and for the door to be opened for him to secure a mortgage loan as a first-time homeowner. The blessing of a house is an easily justifiable request at any stage in one's life, but is the order to be a mortgagee the right one? Have the grounds for your application been limiting God to grant this request via this channel only? What if it is God's desire for you to be debt free? Would it be more targeted to pray for the gift of a house that is already fully paid for, or for an opening to present itself for you to occupy a house, rent and mortgage free, for the rest of your natural life? Is your God incapable of delivering such orders? He is God and has promised that there is no good thing that He will withhold from you who walk uprightly, if you just believe and stop putting yourself in an intercessory tornado. (See Psalm 84:11 KJV.) As God, there is nothing that is impossible for Him to do.

It is time to get out of that prayer spin cycle of begging, doubting, thanking, and disputing; it is time to jump off that spiritual seesaw you have been sitting on and declare that what is yours really is yours; reach for it in the spirit realm, grab it, and do not let go until it manifests in the physical realm. God did not call you to have you lose credibility because of your constant predilection for changing your story or amending what you think He is telling you. He does not tell us 101 different things about our prayer requests before Him; more likely than not, your matter may be adjourned for His decision, and in the interim, self is dictating proceedings and handing down conflicting orders under the guise that it is from the court. Bear in mind that an adjournment of the proceedings is a legitimate part of any court proceedings and being before a heavenly court does not mean that your matter cannot be adjourned for consideration or decision. When a matter is adjourned for decision, be assured that it is being worked on and that God is not in need of any help from you. Sometimes all that is required of you is to stand still: 'And Moses said unto the people, Fear ye not, stand still, and see the salvation of the LORD, which he will shew to you to day: for the Egyptians whom ye have seen to day, ye shall see them again no more for ever. The LORD shall fight for you, and ye shall hold your peace' (Exodus 14:13–14 KJV). Other tools to employ during an adjournment are the weapons of giving thanks, keeping faith, and believing that what you ask for is yours. 'And this is the confidence that we have in him, that, if we ask any thing according to his will, he heareth us: And if we know that he hear us, whatsoever we ask, we know that we have the petitions that we desired of him' (1 John 5:14–15 KJV).

BY PRAYER AND SUPPLICATION

God is calling us to pray precise and targeted prayers, and to become prayer marksmen of finesse, spiritual snipers, and orders experts. So it is important to know where and when to make your application, as well as how to correctly identify the order you are seeking. Then, by prayer and supplication, put your request before Him and ask for the specific order that you want, believing you will receive it. The Word of God asserts that you are to be 'careful for nothing; but in everything **by** prayer and supplication **with** thanksgiving let your requests be made known unto God' (Philippians 4:6 KJV, emphasis added). It is interesting to note here that your approach or way of bringing your case or problem to the heavenly court is 'by prayer and supplication' (which refers to approach) and that this is to be presented 'with thanksgiving'. This clearly suggests that thanksgiving is not an application or means of filing suit but is the attire or dress with which you are adorned when making the application (request or supplication). It accompanies an application but is not the means for bringing it. Likewise, groaning, moaning, crying out, and speaking in tongues are not applications; they are the attire that can be worn when approaching the heavenly court.

A supplication is a petition, request, plea, suit, entreaty, application, or appeal that is placed before the heavenly court in prayer. Yes, it covers an appeal of an order that may be obtained against you. With supplication, it is suggested that your approach is made respectfully and with humility but with an understanding that you have the necessary grounds and right to approach; that is the proper standing for so doing. A supplication covers a plea or entreaty, which is made to set out your case and ask the court to intervene to grant relief. A supplication is not about begging God; it is a legal and spiritual term for making an application or filing suit in a court. So why are Christians engaged in 'begging prayers'? We beg because we refuse to understand that we have standing in the heavenly court and that we must adopt the proper positioning in prayer. We beg because we do not appreciate that our voices have authority, and certainly we know very little about spiritual orders, although we seek and issue them daily. We pray begging prayers because we feel that is how we were taught; they are easy to utter, and we simply do not know better. Likewise, in the earthly court, you must approach respectfully and humbly, once you have a right and the legal grounds to do so, and not by begging, as begging will not give you access to a judge. Many people come to an earthly court when they have reached a breaking point and are in emotional turmoil, but it is not begging prayers (applications) that open the doors of the judicial system to them. Litigants are able to access the court once they have a valid legal ground and the right, having suffered the wrong, to file a suit (claim). Once access is obtained, God calls us to move up to and operate from a higher level of authority (positioning).

This idea of making supplications or putting your applications or appeals against orders entered against you is not new. In the book of Daniel, chapter 6 (KJV), after a decree or ruling is handed down by King Darius barring prayers or petitions being made to any God or man for thirty days except to him, as king, and denying the right of appeal against this order or to have it altered in any way, Daniel takes his case to the heavenly court. The following is written in Daniel 6:10–11 KJV (emphasis mine): 'Now when Daniel knew that the writing was signed, he went into his house; and his windows being open in his chamber toward Jerusalem, he kneeled upon his knees three times a day, and prayed, and gave thanks before his God, as he did aforetime. Then these men assembled, and found Daniel praying and making supplication before his God.' Understand this: when Daniel prayed, he was not begging or pleading for help but must have been operating in the injunctive and restraining mode, because what transpired subsequently pointed to such orders being placed on these lions attacking him.

MONITOR YOUR APPLICATION

God requires that when we bring our application or suit before His heavenly court, we not only make supplication (i.e., present the application, petition, or appeal) but also monitor our application. Put another way, we are to adopt the spirit of a watchman and become spiritual prayer custodians, in order to ensure that our prayer is not dismissed or that an appeal of any decision is required. The Word says, 'Praying always with all <u>prayer and supplication</u> in the Spirit, and <u>watching</u> thereunto with all perseverance and supplication for all saints' (Ephesians 6:18 KJV, emphasis added). You are to be vigilant and become spiritual monitors and watchmen.

Be aware that your application can be dismissed even if it is placed before the right court, even if it is given a hearing, and even if you are on the right side of the law, once the order you are seeking conflicts with or comes via the wrong application. So you cannot pray for physical healing but allow your prayer orders to be a declaration of increased wealth or for a house or just the generalised request of 'bless me Lord, bless me.' Bless you how? The Bible is clear that when you pray, you are to ask for what you want and not for what someone else has. When you ask for what you want, your petition shall be granted. The Bible sets out how to ask and receive; it is clear that you are to come with your request or application in the name of Jesus Christ. (See John 16:24–25 KJV.) Seek and issue the precise order that you want over your situation. This requires you to pray with the mentality and skill of a spiritual marksman, which involves accurate, clear-cut, and direct prayers. To do this, you need to understand the term 'orders', increase your appetite for mastering orders, digest the various types available to you, and be skilled in applying for or issuing them (i.e., become an orders expert). This is no easy hurdle, but it is doable with the help of the Holy Spirit.

WHO CAN SEEK SPIRITUAL ORDERS

In the earthly court, many types of orders are sought and granted on a daily basis. These orders are sought by litigants, whether they are claimants, defendants, third parties, substituted parties, ancillary claimants, or interveners in matters. Yes, you can intervene in a matter and seek an order as someone who is not yet a party to the matter or to protect the interest of a third party. It is much like in the heavenly court, where an intercessor can approach God on behalf of someone else. So here it is important to understand your standing and positioning when you approach the heavenly court. Ask yourself if you are coming as a claimant, defendant, respondent, third party, or an ancillary claimant, applicant, advocate or intervener. Be clear as to your relationship with God and understand your standing – being blood-flushed or blood-washed empowers you to approach from a peculiar and privileged angle. Then know and adopt the correct prayer positioning. When you pray, you are not operating from an earthly court; your position in prayer is spiritual, and so your authority is a heavenly power. That is why I never take my daily commune with God for granted. Sometimes we are muddled in our approach, but a clear and structured approach will always be more effective. We must bear in mind that we are in a battle and a well-structured troop can stand a greater chance of victory than scattered forces.

In addition to your standing or positioning from which you are making this application, you must know of the types of solutions available for your problem and whether your approach is to present a problem or to ward off an attack. This is critical, as it will make for greater accuracy in your prayer life. For instance, if you are under attack, then you would want to assume a defensive stance, apply an order to shield you from the problem, restrain your attacker, and arrest it from continuing to operate in your life. In spiritual warfare, when you are on the defensive on the battlefield, there are many lethal prayer orders that could be applied to disarm, wound, and eradicate your attacker. This is understandable, as in a physical battle there are many weapons; so in spiritual warfare, our weapons are not carnal and certainly not unidimensional. The

Bible speaks of the plurality of spiritual weapons at our disposal, so it is clear that it is not just one weapon with which we enter into spiritual battle. 'For though we walk in the flesh, we do not war after the flesh: (For the <u>weapons</u> of our warfare are not carnal, but mighty through God to the pulling down of strong holds;) Casting down imaginations, and every high thing that exalteth itself against the knowledge of God, and bringing into captivity every thought to the obedience of Christ; And having in a readiness to revenge all disobedience, when your obedience is fulfilled' (2 Corinthians 10:3–6 KJV, emphasis mine).

FORMS OR APPROACHES IN FILING SUIT

There are many approaches to the heavenly court, most of which we are familiar with and already utilise, but I will still discuss a few here.

A PETITION

A petition is a peculiar or unique way of approaching the court, and it is usually used to get a ruling or even pronouncement on something, such as a divorce, clarification of election results, or a call to the bar as an attorney at law. Generally, where a petition is made seeking a ruling – for example, to sever relationship ties – an appeal of that decision is still available. But this manner of approach or moving of the court is suggestive of a softer approach or of the matter being less contested. This is not to say that these matters are not, in many instances, heavily contested or likely to attract injunctive applications. Custody, maintenance, access, financial relief, and property settlements can be quite weighty and heavily contested battles and are all subsumed under the divorce petition, so I am not trying here to minimise these types of matters. It is just that generally, the word 'petition' is more suggestive of a smoother legal journey through the court system.

If your approach is as a petitioner, you may be asking or petitioning the court to move on your behalf to dissolve or untie you from a personal connection with another or to determine an issue that needs clarification (for example, election results). A spiritual petition may be used to request fulfilment of material needs, to sever relationships (soul ties) or treat certain issues in them, or for success in an examination, to name a few uses. It is not that there is no fight in this, but it makes for a different approach and may or may not require a battle line to be drawn. This is also seen where the petition is to be allowed into the legal fraternity to practice law. This is not a warfare supplication; it is simply a petition for access to a profession. Similarly, a petition in the heavenly court does not evoke the element of spiritual warfare, as would, for instance, an application for a restraining order.

AN APPLICATION

Another form for bringing suit is the application, under which a number of matters can be placed before the heavenly court. Applications may be urgent, such as a restraining order, or soft, such as an order for monies to be paid out to you. When coming with an application for injunctive relief or for a restraining order, the approach, the stance, or the attitude to obtain these orders is a fighting one. It is one that requires the applicant to come before the court battle-ready and heavily fortified to ward off bullets and launch lethal attacks. This is explored in greater detail under the subheadings for restraining and injunctive orders. It is just important to understand when to operate in the mode of petitioning or restraining the enemy. Not every prayer is about warfare; some are 'love fests'. By this I mean that there are times when our prayer is about showing God how much we love, appreciate, and are thankful to Him. When we engage in that prayer love tangle with God, there is nothing that can compare with this, for we exit rejuvenated, energised, at peace, strong, and ready to take on the enemy.

A WARRANT

On the opposite extreme of a petition is the approach needed to secure a warrant, of which there are various types. And yes, you can ask for and obtain a spiritual warrant to deal with certain situations, for there are battles you will face where a petition or application will not work and what you need is to issue a warrant to apprehend your enemy. Knowing that there are various types of warrants may also be useful in your warfare.[11]

You may find yourself, in prayer, in pursuit of someone, who may be seeking to abscond or flee the jurisdiction with your property. What you will need in such a case is a fugae warrant, which is capable of pursuing this absconder, removing him from the aeroplane or ship, arresting him, and bringing him before the heavenly court to answer your case against him as to why he is in possession of what belongs to you and refusing to give it up. Then use this order to strip him of your property and retake possession of it. An ordinary warrant of arrest will not work to stop an aeroplane, detain and disembark a passenger, and arrest him in flight from this jurisdiction; only a fugae warrant has that power. You see, it is a different type of battle, so a different solution must be applied.

There are some Christian women who will need to issue fugae warrants or even admiralty orders (not just an ordinary arrest warrant or restraining order) against the women who have taken flight with their husbands; the finances needed by you to take care of your children, your property (car, house, etc.), and your peace of mind and are about to abscond out of the jurisdiction on the vessels of adultery. In certain cases, only a fugae warrant can cause an adulterous offender to disembark from the vessel he or she is using to ride out with your finances, property, possessions, and peace of mind. Only a fugae warrant can be used in some cases to arrest and retake your possessions. An ordinary warrant of arrest does not empower or authorise you to stop an aeroplane from taking off or a ship from sailing. To stop, embark, and remove an adulterous absconder from fleeing the jurisdiction with your property (especially if it is your sole financial source), you will need to use the right instrument or arrest order – namely a fugae warrant or an admiralty order. For example, while a fugae warrant operates to apprehend an absconding debtor who has boarded or is about to embark on an aeroplane out of your jurisdiction, an admiralty order is used to arrest a vessel (ship) and place it in the custody of the marshal of the court until proceedings are determined. It stops the ship from departing the shores and puts it on lockdown.

Apart from the cases above, where an external party approaches for an order, there are instances also when the court moves by its own inherent power to make orders that are sought neither by a claimant nor a defendant. One such order is a dismissal order, which is discussed more below. In the meantime, you are to be aware that while there are many orders available to be sought and obtained, you are to know which one is relevant to solve your particular problem. A few of these orders will be explained in greater detail, but the list is not exhaustive, and it will be simply impossible for me to discuss all of them. With the leading of the Holy Spirit, I have selected a few which I hope will be of utility in the church and bring great relief. These are dealt with in the next chapter, which you should not read or practise without first understanding the divine principles outlined in this chapter. Once you are clear about grounds, standing, positioning, your rights, and the form of an application, as well as how to approach the court, you may move on to read the types of orders available for spiritual warfare.

CHAPTER 6

TYPES OF ORDERS (2)

In this chapter, we will discuss the various types of orders available and practise how to use them effectively as we pray. The aim here is to become fully equipped, trained, and operationalized in the use of spiritual orders. Before moving on to this level, it is advisable that, in preparation, you read the previous chapter on types of orders, for without those foundational divine principles, you will be less of an orders expert. At this stage, you should have an understanding that when you approach the heavenly court, you must have grounds to approach and standing, and you must also know the various types of applications to move the court and know how to adopt the proper positioning in prayer. In this chapter, you are about to learn the types of spiritual orders available to deal with your problems. You are about to become an orders expert.

DISMISSAL ORDER

A dismissal order is one by which the court brings the proceedings to an end or strikes it out of its system. In such a case, the claimant may or may not have a right to bring fresh action; this will be dependent on whether he is still within the statutory period for bringing proceedings in the court. If he is outside of the statutory period, this order effectively brings a permanent end to the matter. It means that a claimant, who ordinarily will have a valid claim, now stands deprived of his remedy. A case may be dismissed at the behest of the court for many reasons, one of which is the failure of a party to take a procedural step or to do an action that is required to keep the matter alive in the court system. The dismissal in such a case is automatic and may be confirmed with a notice being issued to that effect. Another instance in which the court will issue a dismissal order is when it is found that there is no validity in the claim or defence of it before the court. This puts an end to the wasting of the court's time and resources. Dismissal in this case is not automatic but is based on the lack of or deficiency in evidence before the court. A dismissal order is issued against the defendant in cases where his defence is found wanting, deficient, or incapable of answering the claimant's case, meaning that the case is not allowed to stand.

DIVINE AUTOMATIC DISMISSAL

In a similar vein, in the heavenly system, a matter can stand dismissed automatically or for lack of evidence. It is important to note that automatic divine dismissal is not aberrant or whimsical but that it relates always to man's failure to do something. God will not simply dismiss a matter from His consideration by His own volition, even if He has the power to do so. Divine dismissal is automatic because of man's failure to act or take a required step. In other words, it is man's action or omission that operates to attract a dismissal order. The Bible is replete with such examples. One such example was when the people of Israel refused to comply with the instructions of God to enter the rough inhabited terrain of the Amorites and possess the land. They baulked and recoiled from taking the next step because of fear and doubt, even after the report came back favourable and it was in their interest to proceed. (See Deuteronomy 1:20–35 KJV.) This caused a divine automatic dismissal to be issued against them: 'No one from this evil generation shall see the good land I swore to give your ancestors' (Deuteronomy 1:35 NIV). The effect of this divine dismissal was to shut out the disobedient Israelites and those without faith from His heavenly court and leave them vulnerable to the attacks of their enemies. It was to effectively deny them a hearing by God: 'And ye returned and wept before the

LORD; but the LORD would not hearken to your voice, nor give ear unto you' (Deuteronomy 1: 45 KJV).

Another very graphic demonstration of the issuing of a divine automatic dismissal is contained in the story of Noah. In this story, stubbornness and refusal to listen to God, to heed His warnings to repent, and to take a procedural step that would lead to salvation resulted in persons being shut out from the ark. It was, in effect, God pronouncing an execution order in the form of a divine automatic dismissal. (See Genesis 7:16–23 KJV.)

What is important for you to understand is that there *must* be a reason for a dismissal order to be issued by the court, whether it is a divine automatic dismissal or a dismissal for deficient evidence. The court, by issuing this notice of dismissal, is simply saying that you have not done what was required to be done and the time has expired for you to act, so the court's hands are now tied, and, therefore, your matter stands dismissed. Despite this, you retain a right in any matter that you have before God to influence or determine its outcome and to avoid getting a divine automatic dismissal. It is here that the concept of giving thanks always and in everything becomes important, because thanksgiving is a step; it is a reminder to God that you have not forgotten your supplication (whether in the form of a petition, request, application, or appeal) that has been placed before Him. Expressing thanks has the power to keep your request alive before Him and to protect you from attracting a divine dismissal order. Giving thanks is a procedural step that God never gets tired of, which means that you can do this daily, every hour and every minute. If you think of it as a reminder to God that your application is before Him, you will want to do this often.

Another critical step is praise and worship; this should be done continually. Praise and worship is not just a procedural step, which has the power of keeping your matter continually in the face of God; it is an initiating, interim, and final step (so you can do it before presenting your request, while your matter is before the court and after your order is granted). Yet another divine principle of relevance is that of the longsuffering nature of God, but 'longsuffering' does not mean 'permanently suffering'. There comes a time when divine steps will be taken to execute judgment or put an end to the matter, despite the longsuffering nature of God. (See Exodus 7; 12:29–30 and 14:26–28 KJV.) A few other divine principles to keep your matter alive before God include fasting, tithing, and faith. There is a power contained in faith – that expectant waiting before the heavenly court to make its pronouncement while holding steadfastly to His promises – which has the capacity to move God to act. He is moved to act simply on your belief and faith that it will come to pass and never be dismissed. As Christians, we understand this concept. It is Abraham's kind of faith that will operate to wall off a dismissal order or shield you from it – not diluted, wavering, and wobbly faith.

When you are praying for a long time and the answer is not forthcoming, check whether your matter has been dismissed. Stop treating a dismissed matter as if it were live proceedings still before the heavenly court. See whether you are still within time to revive the matter and whether you should be praying to restore it (by appeal), make an application to amend your request or extend the time to do what you were required to do, or refile (or reapply) for a different order to solve your problems. Become a sniper Christian – sharp, precise, on the offensive, and ready to take out the enemy. Do not allow him to attack first, and if it happens, move to reverse and revoke or set aside the attack.

DIVINE DISMISSAL FOR REASON OR A SEASON

On the other hand, dismissal for want of evidence means that the court has considered your case and it come up deficient and must fail. Such a dismissal occurs for a reason, but dismissal can also occur for a season. Where divine dismissal is for a reason, it is a more permanent solution. There are times when we pray for certain things and our application or petition is not granted and we are confused. We will not get everything we pray for, because sometimes it may not be in our interest to be granted our request. If your request is permanently denied (for example, for a failure to prove your case) this falls under a dismissal for reason or cause. Your matter can only be brought back if it is appealed and the dismissal order is reversed. Learn to recognise when your matter is dismissed outright (for reason) or denied for a period (for a season).

On the other hand, dismissal for a season is a temporary reality. It may just be that the grant of your request is delayed or fixed for another time. (See Daniel 10:11–13 KJV.) The Bible speaks about seasons; for everything there is a season and time, so check whether that season has passed or whether you are still going through it. (See Ecclesiastes 3:1 KJV.) A spiritual marksman will not miss his timing or season, but how many of us have the praying skill and mentality of a sniper, allowing us to hit our targets every time? Dismissal for a season is equated to the legal concept of adjournment. In court, we use the term 'adjourn', which is simply our way of saying that the order you are seeking is being put off to be granted on another date. It is the same way in the heavenly court. God operates by seasons and not according to our timing. In such instances, we are assured that our request is considered, but not granted, as of this time; or further consideration of the evidence is required; or God wants us to apply for a different and better order. It is important to know whether the dismissal is for a season or a reason.

A perfect example where a dismissal was issued for

a season occurred prior to me getting the current job that I have. At that time, I knew I had to vacate the job I was doing, for my spiritual tenure for occupying that seat had expired. God even confirmed this to me through a word of prophecy that He would open a door for me to get a different position, so I began to apply for any job opening that came up. Needless to say, I began receiving dismissal after dismissal, and as the doors kept being shut in my face, the doubts came as to whether I had heard right. Then, when I least expected it, God opened the door for my present job (one that I had always wanted but thought was beyond my reach), and it was a higher and more financially lucrative position than all the others for which I had been applying. It showed me that my dismissal from those downstream employment positions was not for a reason (such as a lack of readiness or qualification for promotion); it was for a season. That temporary, or seasonal, dismissal worked in my favour by facilitating me to get a better position.

Learn to recognise when your matter is dismissed for a season or reason; also, if it has been adjourned, learn what that means. Sometimes your matter is adjourned for a short or long period, which means it has a fixed date to come back before the court; or it may be adjourned generally, which is a term of art that means no fixed date is given for the next hearing but you are required to take a step to bring it back before the court. In effect, it is placed in the court's suspense docket. That is, during that period of suspension, there is no live consideration being given to your matter. There are certain adjournments that result in your matter being worked on by God behind the scenes. Some of you may have this confirmed by God through prophecy, where you would be told He is working things out for you but others may just face silence. His silence does not mean that God has stopped working on your problems. It is your faith that will take you through your periods of adjournments, so pray for sharpened spiritual insight and increased perception. When you find you are praying for a specific thing or about an ongoing and intractable problem in your life and not getting a breakthrough, check to see if you are being dismissed for a reason or a season.

ISSUING DIVINE DISMISSAL ORDERS

Apart from the court operating on its own initiative to dismiss a case, you can move the court to have a matter dismissed. Or you can issue dismissal orders against the works of the enemy in your life or someone else's life. When doing so, it is advisable to issue dismissal orders for a reason, which is a more permanent fix, rather than for a season. Practising and becoming skilled in the issuance of dismissal orders over your life and the lives of your family members are critical. Many Christians already issue such orders over their lives – for example, dismissing generational curses, diseases, or negative words pronounced against your Christian walk or professional progress. I want to bolster this practice of issuing divine dismissal orders by recommending the need for precision even in the making of such orders.

A dismissal order contains an active ingredient. By this I mean that it is not as if you are making a declaration, which is static or fixed, but that it is more in the nature of an enforcement order. It is a means of bringing closure or putting an end to proceedings. It means your dismissal or words are injected with the power of enforcement; they are charged with energy and are capable of taking effect immediately on pronouncement to terminate a situation. So if you are praying for a situation to be dismissed from your life, do so with the understanding that as soon as you issue that dismissal notice, that thing or situation is vanquished, gone, done – eliminated. A dismissal for cause or reason by the earthly court is permanent, not seasonal, so it evaporates the problem. Similarly, a divine automatic dismissal for reason is permanent and effectively discharges or removes the problem. Do not dismiss a situation and then continue to pray for God to help you with it; understand, on issue of this notice, that it is done.

A dismissal order is a final order; it is not interim in nature, so do not continue to revive the matter or treat it as if it were still in existence. Part of our problem is a lack of understanding when we pray. It makes sense if you think of it like this: if a matter is dismissed and you continue to bring it back before the heavenly court, what you are in effect doing is reviving it and asking God to reconsider His dismissal of that problem and continue to treat it as a live issue. In effect, you are seeking a reinstatement order, so this allows your problem to continue. By continuing to pray about the problem after a dismissal notice has been issued, you are saying to God, 'Give me permission to set aside that dismissal order. You see, I still need to put some prayers on this problem; I'm not finished with it yet, Lord; I still have some spiritual blows to pelt on it. So I make an appeal to restore my problem and seek an extension of time from You, God, to continue to allow this problem to plague my life and to pray some more to get rid of it.' This may explain why some Christians are caught up in the cycle of dismissing and restoring matters, meaning they will never get resolution to their problems. Then we blame God and wonder if we heard right that a particular problem had been dealt with and dismissed from our lives. For too long, we have sabotaged our own prayers and undercut our deliverances. Stop being spiritual saboteurs.

Let us issue a dismissal order in prayer:

> Thank You, God, for giving me the understanding and equipping me with the

tools to deal with all situations that arise in my life. Today I place before You this [name problem] that has been ongoing in my life for far too long without resolution. I confess that by my words, thoughts, and actions, I have fed it, energised it, bolstered it, held on to it, and so allowed it to keep me in a stranglehold. But no more, Lord; today I seek and issue a dismissal notice against [name the problem] and say directly to it that *it is over, done, ended – dismissed*. You, [name problem], have been exposed, stripped, weakened, and destroyed, and your case has been found wanting and without any basis to continue to stand. No longer will you continue to interfere with my peace, threaten my security, and steal my joy. No longer will you be a source of frustration, oppression, and depression. I denounce you, undress you, and weaken whatever prior hold you had on me that caused you to continue manifesting in my life. As of today, you shall manifest no more in my life, for I drive you out and command you to enter into and be drowned in the Indian Ocean. Your hold on my life is broken, stifled, and suffocated, and you are summarily dismissed. You will not be revived, restored, or reinstated, because this dismissal notice is sufficient to eradicate you from my life completely. This dismissal notice is stamped and sealed with the blood of Jesus Christ and now stands enforced as a final order of His heavenly court. There is no energy or life left in you to do me (or my family) any harm. You, [problem], are dismissed, and I remove, deprive, and bar you from any right of appeal or reinstatement in this matter, in the name of Jesus Christ. Amen.

DECLARATORY ORDER

A declaratory order is an affirmation or confirmation of what obtains. It is the single most potent and unshakeable pronouncement of the court. It does not, by its issuance, seek to change a situation, alter the status quo, make an amendment, or put an interim position in place. It is simply the court pronouncing that something is what it is. For example, man cannot by his own will change the fact that there is a sun that shines overhead; a declaration to that effect is indisputable. It is an incontrovertible statement and one that is fixed and unquestionable. It is much like the biblical statements by God that 'I AM THAT I AM' (Exodus 3:14 KJV) and 'I am Alpha and Omega, the beginning and the ending, saith the Lord, which is, and which was, and which is to come, the Almighty' (Revelation 1:8 KJV). Yet another declaratory pronouncement was uttered when Jesus stated, 'Verily, verily, I say unto you,

Before Abraham was, I am' (John 8:58 KJV). These are declaratory pronouncements by God that say who He is and that this is just how it is; it is not up for or capable of challenge.

When God asserts, 'I AM THAT I AM', He has, in fact, issued a declaratory order which speaks to the immutable, unassailable, unquestionable, undeniable nature of God. Man may question it, not believe it, deny it, or even seek to refute it, but it is what it is; God is the 'I AM THAT I AM'. The Bible starts off with a declaratory statement: 'In the beginning God created the heaven and the earth' (Genesis 1 KJV), followed by a series of commands. There must be a reason for the God who is order to start off with a declaratory order backed up by commands. As creator, He was ordering the world to take shape and to be order, even as He is order. Okay, hold up; take a deep breath. Why was it important for God to start off with a declaratory order? Because He is order. He was placing in order His world with His Word, who is His Son, Jesus Christ, as the symbol of order in the world. Does this sound confusing? Then read the first chapter of Genesis and see if it is not a declaration as to who God is, what He did, and what obtains as an incontrovertible truth.

It is critical that we pray declaratory prayers over our lives and our children's lives. A declaration says that it is what it is. This means that no man or demon can interfere with or alter a declaration. There are many promises of God in His Word for which we need to seek declaratory orders. If we desire to have these promises, then we must issue declaratory orders, with the understanding that these are unshakeable. We need to declare what we would have manifested in our lives, with the understanding of the potency of such a pronouncement. So it is irrelevant what is manifesting or whether your authority is being questioned. When a declaratory order is issued, it puts a halt to the doubts, the attacks, the questioning, and the undermining, because it establishes and affirms a position, rendering it unshakeable and unalterable. 'But he answered and said, It is written, Man shall not live by bread alone, but by every word that proceedeth out of the mouth of God' (Matthew 4:4 KJV). (See also Matthew 4:7, 10 KJV.)

If a court order declares that you are the owner of a piece of land, then that is all that is required for you to act or take steps as the owner of that land. It is the type of order that is made in divorce proceedings, together with the decree which severs the legal relationship, but its power lies in its affirmation or declaration that the legal relationship ties are effectively cut. The declaratory aspect of a divorce decree is not intended to sever the relationship cords but to affirm, confirm, and pronounce the cut, end, or dissolution of the marriage as being so (discussed further below). So, as Christians, we are to issue declaratory orders over our lives. For example: 'I declare that this is my job, promotion is mine, and all obstacles to my professional advancement are removed. You may be in occupation of my chair now, but I declare that it is mine; and your temporary occupation is just that – an interim state of affairs. I declare that that chair is mine, and you are removed from occupying it, in the name of Jesus Christ. In fact, I enter into the spirit realm and move it from its current position and place it in my preferred sitting position in my office that you temporarily occupy, because I like the view from here better.' We must issue declaratory prayers, and it is our failure to do so that has been hindering our progress in certain situations or preventing us from getting what we want.

To make it clear, when a declaratory order is issued, it is never qualified; nor does it come with an addendum or ultimatum. Hear me clearly; a declaratory order is never qualified by the words 'if it is your will, Lord', which inject an element of doubt and uncertainty. If you are making a declaratory order, it is understood that it is in or by the will of God, and once it is God's will for your life, there is no need to add that addendum or qualification or what we term a caveat to such an order. Caveats do not apply to declaratory orders in law.

A declaratory order proclaims what the true state of affairs is; it pronounces the truth of a thing. There is no qualification of the truth, for truth *is*. So when you are praying and making such a pronouncement, there is no need to beg, whine, plead, grovel, put a caveat on your request, or seek to justify it; simply declare what is. A declaration is the most forceful, unchallengeable, unassailable, incontestable, unanswerable statement of a truth. Some situations will never change until you begin to make declaratory orders over them. There are many promises contained in the Bible that we need to start using as declaratory orders over our lives and our children's lives.

Here are a few such declaratory orders that we can make over our loved ones' lives and ours, during prayer:

	Biblical Declaration	Application of Declaratory Order
1.	The steps of a good man are ordered by the Lord: and he delighteth in his way. Though he fall, he shall not be utterly cast down: for the Lord upholdeth him with his hand. (Psalm 37:23–24 KJV)	I declare that my steps are ordered by God and He takes pleasure in them. God holds me to prevent me from falling flat on my face.

Biblical Declaration	Application of Declaratory Order
2. Thou preparest a table before me in the presence of mine enemies: thou anointest my head with oil; my cup runneth over. (Psalm 23:5 KJV)	I declare that God has prepared a banquet table before me on which is laid out every conceivable food and drink, in full view of my enemies. He then anointed my head with overflowing oils of blessings and is causing my cup of possessions to flow over its top, so that I have no lack in my life.
3. And they shall fight against thee; but they shall not prevail against thee; for I am with thee, saith the Lord, to deliver thee. (Jeremiah 1:19 KJV)	I declare over my life and those of my children that my enemies who fight me will never prevail against me, for my God stands with and fights for me to deliver me out of their hands.

Biblical Declaration	Application of Declaratory Order
4. For the Lord your God is he that goeth with you, to fight for you against your enemies, to save you. (Deuteronomy 20:4 KJV)	I issue a declaratory cover of protection over my life and pronounce that God goes before me to fight my enemies and to save me.
5. See, I have this day set thee over the nations and over the kingdoms, to root out, and to pull down, and to destroy, and to throw down, to build, and to plant. (Jeremiah 1:10 KJV)	I declare that God has placed me above nations, kingdoms, and continents and vested me with the power to pull down, destroy, and root up the works of darkness, and He has given me authority to build, plant, and make a fresh start.

Biblical Declaration	Application of Declaratory Order
6. God is not a man, that he should lie; neither the son of man, that he should repent: hath he said, and shall he not do it? or hath he spoken, and shall he not make it good? (Numbers 23:19 KJV)	I declare that when God speaks it is so, for He is not a man so that He would lie; whatever He says shall come to pass. He says that my [job, children, house, etc.] is mine, so it is mine, and I take possession of this [position/property].
7. That at the name of Jesus every knee should bow, of things in heaven, and things in earth, and things under the earth; And that every tongue should confess that Jesus Christ is Lord, to the glory of God the Father. (Philippians 2:10–11 KJV)	I declare that the Word of God is truth and must come to pass. It says that every man and thing in heaven, on earth, or below the earth will bow at the name of Jesus and every tongue shall confess that Jesus Christ is Lord, in glory to God the Father.

Biblical Declaration	Application of Declaratory Order
8. Behold, I give unto you power to tread on serpents and scorpions, and over all the power of the enemy: and nothing shall by any means hurt you. (Luke 10:19 KJV)	God has given me power to step on and trample snakes and scorpions and every dark manifestation or work of Satan, and I declare that nothing shall harm or hurt me.
9. The righteous eateth to the satisfying of his soul: but the belly of the wicked shall want. (Proverbs 13:25 KJV)	I declare that I shall have no want or lack for provision, but the wicked shall be without sustenance.
10. I am fearfully and wonderfully made: marvellous are thy works; ... How precious also are thy thoughts unto me, O God! how great is the sum of them! (Psalm 139:14, 17 KJV)	I declare that I am a marvellous masterpiece of God who was wonderfully and beautifully made. God thinks that I am precious and a treasure of His.

Biblical Declaration	Application of Declaratory Order
11. The adversaries of the LORD shall be broken to pieces; out of heaven shall he thunder upon them: the LORD shall judge the ends of the earth; and he shall give strength unto his king, and exalt the horn of his anointed. (1 Samuel 2:10 KJV)	I declare and proclaim into the atmosphere that the enemies of Jesus shall be destroyed and broken into small pieces and that God will rumble and roar at them out of heaven and judge the earth but shall give strength to and exalt his anointed ones, of which I am one.
12. 'For I know the plans I have for you' declares the Lord, 'plans to prosper you and not to harm you, plans to give you hope and a future.' (Jeremiah 29:11 NIV)	I declare that God has plans for my life – plans that will cause me to prosper and not bring harm, and plans to give me hope and an enlarged future.

Biblical Declaration	Application of Declaratory Order
13. For with God nothing shall be impossible. (Luke 1:37 KJV) Ah Lord GOD! behold, thou hast made the heaven and the earth by thy great power and stretched out arm, and there is nothing too hard for thee. (Jeremiah 32:17 KJV)	God can do all things; there is nothing that is impossible for Him to do. There is not anything that is too difficult for God to accomplish. All things are possible with God.

INJUNCTIVE ORDER

An injunctive order has the effect of moving the court to pronounce the fastest in any matter. It is usually sought in cases of urgency or emergency and forces the court to immediately grant a hearing and make a ruling. It matters not what time of day or night or even if the court is otherwise engaged or on vacation. The court must stop, return, reconvene, and give judicial consideration to the issue. It reaches the ear of a judge immediately upon being filed or even before documents are fully drafted. These types of applications are shepherded or hovered over by officers of the court, from beginning to end. It means that once the court gets word that an injunctive application is to be filed, the wheels of justice begin to prepare themselves to receive it. An injunctive order is awarded in circumstances: when not all the evidence is before the court, when (if not granted) the person would suffer irreversible or irreparable injury for which he would not have any adequate remedy in law, when the court must balance the hardship of granting as against not giving an injunction, and when it would not operate against public interest. It is generally interim in nature but can, after all the evidence has been brought before the court, be pronounced as a final order.

You may ask why it is necessary to seek an injunctive order when you can simply go for a final order. Such an order is not only necessary but is also critical to apply for. In fact, in any judicial system, it is one of the most sought after orders to put a speedy halt to a problem. By its very nature, it comes with the full force and authority of the entire judicial system, with an immediacy and power that bear no questioning or resistance to it taking instant hold. This is the order that is used to put an abrupt stop to any unlawful or questionable decision, action, or activity and to bring the dispute immediately before the court. It is a lockdown order, a cease-and-desist order, or a maintenance-of-the-status-quo order until the court says further. In certain cases, just the mere mention of an injunctive order being granted or even being sought can have the effect of getting compliance during a disturbance. It is one of the most powerful and effective tools available in the court system, and it tolerates no defiance. It is usually referred to as the 'slapping of an injunction' against someone, which implies the bringing of that person to heel, or to his full senses, until the court has time to hear the evidence or parties. Important to understand is that the order is usually applied for ex parte – that is, without serving the other side notice to attend the hearing, because of its urgency.

There are issues in our lives that, when we pray, are so urgent that we must slap an injunction against the offending party to immediately halt what is taking place. When an injunctive order is applied, it is irrelevant who the person or company is, how much money or authority he or it holds, or even if it is the government; he or it must stop immediately. Such an order is served with a penal clause imprinted on it in red; this warns the person served that if he does not stop immediately, he will be subject to imprisonment. There are certain intractable problems that will not stop bleeding in our lives unless we slap injunctive orders on them. Bear in mind that when your situation is urgent or is bordering on or has reached crisis, an injunctive order may become necessary. Once this application is placed before the heavenly court, all of the entire angelic hosts have a shepherd's responsibility over this application. They do not cease to hover and cover this application and to see it through until the injunctive order is enforced.

It is utilised where you have a burning problem from which you need instant release. And it brings immediate relief to the problem. We do not get immediate relief if we do not seek an injunctive order. It is time that Christians move from begging prayers and understand their authority in Christ Jesus to seek injunctive relief. Injunctive relief is more than just bringing a petition before God; it is a loud clarion call that wakes up the hosts of heaven, marshalling the entire heavenly system in preparation for it and forces God to act immediately to send relief.

I remember when God first ministered to me to place certain issues under an injunctive order and because I understood the force, respect, and immediacy of this power, I began to order injunctions against ongoing issues in my life. The reliefs were swift and effective to nail down some painful issues, to the extent that I found myself wanting to operate only in the injunctive mode. Then He reminded me that I should know better because an injunctive order is not to be lightly sought or applied; these orders are reserved for serious cases and not every single problem in my life. He reminded me of the need to pray precisely and not to misuse my prayer tools. For in a court of law, if you seek an injunctive order when it is not the right means of approaching the court, you may be shut down or dismissed for lack of urgency and subject to a loss of credibility. Injunctive proceedings are best suited when there is unwarranted interference with a person's rights and when, if an urgent hearing is not convened, the person stands a chance of losing everything. It arises when a person is at risk of being left without compensation or of having no further opportunity for any remedy, or when it is necessary to preserve the status quo. It is for serious cases. Remember: if it is misused, you will lose credibility and standing. If it is applied for erroneously and refused, it weakens your case going forward, so this is not a procedure to use glibly or lightly. Remember: not every prayer should seek injunctive relief; it is applicable for only certain serious cases.

Following is an example of how to release an injunctive order during prayer:

> Father, Your power and greatness are beyond question or challenge, for You are omnipotent. When You speak or utter Your command, there is nothing and no one in heaven or earth or hell who can rise up to defy Your ruling. I seek an urgent prohibition order of You, for this problem, [name problem], besets, harasses, annoys, and overwhelms me. I seek injunctive relief and thank You for Your swift response and for the angelic hosts who are right now preparing to deliver and enforce this order. By the power that You have vested in me, through Jesus Christ, I now apply (pronounce or proclaim) an interim

injunction against you [name problem or person] and steamroll any further progress of you in my life and impact on my peace. I slap this injunction on you, restraining, prohibiting, preventing, stopping, barring, and halting you, your agents, your cohorts, and your operatives from interfering with, obstructing, or placing obstacles in my path, or from stymying my progress. With immediate effect, I apply the blood of Jesus Christ to this order, to restrain, restrict, prevent, and exclude you, [name problem or person], from intimidating, harassing, and threatening me [or name the person] whether by words, by thoughts, or by actions.

You, your agents, and your henchmen are barred, restrained, and prohibited from coming within 100 feet of my family or me, or from entering my space – full stop. You are mandated to comply and obey this order, as it is stamped and sealed with the blood of Christ Jesus and the fire of the Holy Ghost. Operate now, Holy Ghost fire, to burn and purge away any steps likely to be taken in opposition to this injunction. It remains in force and continues against you, devil, until I notify you of a further order or hearing date, so you are now subject to my control. All power to impact my peace is now ceded to me, and I whip you into order. Your steps, your words, your actions, and your thoughts that previously harassed and threatened my life are brought into subjection and vaporised. You will not, without the permission of this heavenly court, act contrarily to or adversely to my best interest in this matter, for you are rendered powerless and placed in a comatose state until I say [or 'God says'] otherwise. You will not be able to disobey this order, and any attempt to do so will attract further penalties and put you in peril of losing your freedom, property, and assets, in the name of Jesus. Amen.

RESTRAINING ORDER

Many Christians will be familiar with the term 'restraining order', but do they know exactly what it means or understand why this is an order that attracts defiance more than any other? Do they understand why, when we utter prayers to restrain persons from acting in a particular manner, without more, that it triggers a reaction? A restraint seeks to harness behaviour and restricts freedom so people lash out when such restrictions are placed on them. It is normal if one is tied down to struggle to be released; that is why restraining orders attract retaliation. A restraining order is a spiritual block or spiritual death knell, so when such an order is made in your prayer life, you must put other blockers in place. You must expect reaction and seek to put systems or spiritual blocks in place to treat with this. This is why in the court system a restraining order goes hand in hand with an injunctive order; they fortify and buttress each other.

Restraining and injunctive orders are similar by nature, with the restraining order being a type of injunction which is usually given to preserve the status quo, bar further acts of trespass or entry unto land, and prevent stalking, sexual harassment, domestic violence, and harassment. Both orders are used to *prohibit* misconduct and *mandate* a required conduct, so they are termed 'prohibitory injunctions' and 'mandatory injunctions'. The distinction lies more in application than substance, but there is a tendency for a spirit of escalation and reaction to come when a restraining order is applied, more so than an injunction. This may be so because the restraining order implies or suggests the physical tying down, shackling, or holding down of a person by putting a restraint on him. It suggests a deprivation of freedom but more so a restriction of physical movement.

They are both interim reliefs, so we must understand that they are temporary in nature and a more permanent order is required. They are important as first steps to halt the progress of undesirable behaviours, actions, or decisions that place you in jeopardy or threaten your life, but they are not permanent fixes. Because a restraining order is not initially a permanent fix to a problem, this does not mean that it is not to be sought. In fact, this is critical, because it too provides fast relief and is easy to obtain in a court system; therein lies its usefulness until the more permanent or final solution is granted. When you need to restrain a person from acting in a particular manner, to tie his behaviour, to disrupt his action, stymie his movements – this is a useful tool. Once this is done, the more permanent fix of a judgment order can be applied. Incorporated in this final judgment order is the making permanent of the injunctive or restraining order. The major benefit of this lies in the immediacy of the relief obtained, and it can also be useful as a warning to the errant that more deadly blows will follow if one does not stop.[12]

Here is how you can apply a restraining order on your situation during prayer:

> You, [name the problem], are hereby barred, tied down, restricted, prevented, and restrained from acting as you have been. I forbid, bind, and shackle you from continuing your attack. Your unlawful trespass unto and attempts to seize and assume ownership of my property end now. I dismantle and weaken your weapons and place you under a restraining order, which takes immediate effect. You are not to come close to me, enter my space, lay hands on me, stalk me,

communicate with my family members or me, or even speak my name. Your destructive words and actions, as well as your harassing behaviour, are to cease now, for they have been rendered null and void in the face of this order. All attempts by you to rise up, resist, fight against this restraint, or escalate this matter are blocked, walled off, and nailed down. You are no longer able to threaten, harass, or intimidate my life. This restraining order is in effect, having been sealed with the blood of Jesus Christ, and will not be set aside. I deny you the right to apply to lift it or bar its continuation, in the name of Jesus Christ. Amen.

ARREST ORDER

There are some problems in your life which must first be placed under an arrest order before a final sentence can be passed. Everyone knows what it means to arrest someone, but I will still explain this concept. A warrant of arrest is a document that empowers the person in whose name it is issued to stop the person to whom it is directed, take him into the custody of the police force, and so effectively deprive him of his liberty. He is locked up, put away, and jailed until his day comes for a trial, to determine whether he should be convicted or set free. Well, if the legal system is like the one that exists in my country, he may never taste freedom. Sometimes all that is required to deal with certain problems is to arrest them, which means that you have put a stop to them and locked them up. By depriving your problem of the ability to continue accessing you and invading your space, you may get the solution for it. Some arrestees are entitled to bail, so in prayer be careful to close up this loophole and ensure that this is refused. Sometimes you may need to go a step further and actually convict and sentence the problem to life in prison so that it does not affect you anymore. If necessary, you may want to simultaneously place a death penalty sentence on this problem and proceed to deny it of any right of appeal but move quickly to place the hangman's noose around its neck.

Breaking the neck of a miscreant is no longer a popular practice in modern society, but in spiritual warfare, it is an apt punishment to execute. In fact, it was the punishment meted out to Eli for his sin: 'And the messenger answered and said, Israel is fled before the Philistines, and there hath been also a great slaughter among the people, and thy two sons also, Hophni and Phinehas, are dead, and the ark of God is taken. And it came to pass, when he made mention of the ark of God, that he fell from off the seat backward by the side of the gate, and his neck brake, and he died: for he was an old man, and heavy. And he had judged Israel forty years' (1 Samuel 4:17–18 KJV).

When issuing an execution order, I will literally picture the hangman's noose being draped around the deviant's neck and the trap door opening, swiping off the neck of my problem. In a spiritual battle, you must be prepared to be spiritual hangmen and willing and able to move in for the spiritual kill. If you are not capable of executing the judgment or completing the act, then do not utilise this weapon, for it is for the strong of heart and the person in right standing and operating from the correct positioning.

Let me explain so you appreciate that this execution order is for persons who are at the spiritual level to, and have the skill to, pray lethal prayers and so secure the spiritual demise of certain problems. In 1999 in Trinidad and Tobago, a gang of notorious, murderous drug-trafficking men, in all nine, under death sentences, were placed in the care of a female judicial officer responsible for carrying out the order of the court. It was decided by this officer that she would carry out the execution by hanging over a period of three days, executing three men on each day. On the first day of the execution, she prepared herself to carry out the court's order by hanging the gang leader first. As the first condemned prisoner received his punishment, the woman nearly fainted, slumping weakly against the shoulder of her deputy, and was unable to carry out her functions of executing the rest of the men. If you are incapable of issuing a hangman's order or carrying out the function, then stick to prayers that are more suited to your level of spiritual maturity. Do not seek to carry out a hangman's order if your spiritual constitution is not up to it. Stop at the arrest and sentencing of your problem for life; you may even throw away the key if it makes you feel better, but do not seek to execute a death sentence on your problem if you do not have the spiritual maturity to do so. There is a responsibility that comes with the exercise of this type of lethal warfare, and you must know how to attire yourself with spiritual garments to protect you from the consequences of praying at that particular level.

Following is an example of issuing an arrest warrant and conviction (not a death sentence) in prayer:

> I come boldly into Your presence, in no other name but the name of Jesus Christ. The name of Jesus Christ is higher than any other name on earth that I can turn to, so I bring my request for relief before You, in His name. I confess that I have been wrestling and holding at bay this problem (name problem), but my energies are now spent, and I am weary from my pursuit. I ask for this problem to be arrested and brought before Your court to answer why it has been threatening my peace, security, and life. This warrant of arrest is directed to you, [name], and puts you under my control. I place these spiritual

handcuffs on your hands and shackle you to my side, for my benefit and peace of mind. By this warrant, your movements are restricted and freedom denied; you are dependent on me for sustenance and life, and I deprive you of both, for I will not feed you to enable you to continue tormenting me. I throw you into a cell and lock it, sealing you off from doing any further mischief and sealing you off from escape. You are not permitted to bring any application for bail, and if perchance by subterfuge you slip one out, I release custodian angels to stand guard and intercept any such bail requests and deny them now. I abridge the time for you to appear before the heavenly court, and I ask for and secure a conviction against you, by which you are now sentenced to life in prison without the possibility of parole or bail. I also seal you off from being able to secure any presidential pardon. You will occupy a tiny jail cell, with no airing time allowed, where you will remain until you depart this life, in Jesus' name I pray. Amen.

PROTECTION ORDER

In our jurisdiction, a protection order is a variant of a restraining order but deals specifically with the protection of the individual, in the context of domestic violence matters. It covers protection for individuals in relationships, whose lives are under threat. A protection order gives the police an immediate right of arrest on breach, unlike with a restraining order, under which the applicant will be required to return to the court to get permission to enforce the contempt order. A restraining order is also of wider scope; it covers other matters, such as trespass on land and other property. A protection order is specific to an individual seeking legal fortification or shield in domestic violence cases.

There are many situations in your life that need to be placed under protection orders. So it is important to understand when these are obtained and how to most effectively apply for and effect these. Protection orders are daily requests made of God by Christians. Sometimes it is done in a mindless, effortless, secondary way, but be aware that seeking God's protection over our lives, family members' lives, possessions, travels, finances, health, and so forth is no simple or secondary matter. It is a serious request. We tend to appreciate how protected we are, or how in need of protection we are, only when we come under attack. This is an area in our lives that we take for granted.

Recently I was told a story of a young lady who was busy living her life for herself, aware of God but unconcerned about serving Him. She was asked by a cousin of hers to accompany him to collect some money at night time from some men in a neighbouring village.

He begged her to use her car for the journey, and on the way, he received a call asking for his location and the type and colour of car he was driving. Without identifying that he was not the driver, he gave the information, ignoring her protestation about giving out those details. After a few minutes of driving along the dark road, a vehicle came into her path and blocked her car, spraying it with bullets. She stopped, and the gunman ran up, pointed the gun at her in the driver's seat, and pulled the trigger, but it was blocked. She managed to escape into the bushes, her cousin having already made his escape, as the incident unfolded. As she ran for her life, she was unaware that she had been shot in the back and had picked up a few more bullets as she escaped. She found herself in the yard of someone whose help she sought to contact the police. She was seriously wounded but escaped with her life. On her hospital bed, she began to thank her sisters, who were always praying for her protection, and finally acknowledged that it was God who was protecting her and that she needed to change her life to live for Him. It takes a tragedy sometimes for God to get one's attention, but it shows how a protection order can safeguard the life of your loved ones. A protection order is not to be issued mindlessly, for it saves lives.

HABEAS CORPUS ORDER

A habeas corpus order is sought to bring a person who is under arrest before a judge or into court. The summons or application specifically requires the arrested person to be presented bodily or physically before the court. It is used especially for the purpose of acquiring the person's release unless lawful reasons can be shown for keeping him detained. The term habeas corpus comes from the mediaeval Latin "heɪbiəs 'kɔːrpəs' and literally means 'You may have the body.' It is a tool to fight off illegal imprisonment or confinement by demanding that a prisoner, patient, or someone unlawfully deprived of his freedom be taken before the court, and that the custodian provide the proof of authority for having him imprisoned. It allows the court to have oversight into and determine for itself whether the hospital administration or prison authorities have the lawful authority to detain the prisoner. If the custodian is acting beyond his authority, then the prisoner must be released. It is known as being the recourse utilised by the cruellest, meanest, or vilest amongst us, against the mightiest and the holders of power in society. In reality, of course, it is a remedy that any person who finds himself deprived unlawfully of his freedom can use to get instantaneous judicial oversight in his matter. It is a remedy available in cases where a person is being held in secret or is unlawfully detained. Habeas corpus has certain limitations, as it is theoretically only an interim or procedural remedy. In effect, it guards against unlawful imprisonment, unwarranted and illegal restrictions, or detainment; but it does not necessarily protect other rights, such as your entitlement to a fair trial.

There are instances when a Christian may need to issue a habeas corpus order to have the body of a family member, which may be under the control of bad influences or notorious persons, released and brought before the heavenly court to free that person from the hold of sin. As Christians, we know that there is no distance with prayer, but sometimes a habeas corpus prayer, which commands the release of a physical stranglehold or confinement of a loved one by others, may be a trigger to having him set free from the bonds of sin. This is an effective tool or key for unlocking prison cells of drugs, gang activity, sexual perversion, alcoholism, and other vices that may be holding your loved ones imprisoned. There are some intractable problems that may be dealt with or removed through the use of this order such as mental illness, cult membership, or generational curses. Understand that once a habeas corpus order is issued, it must be complied with immediately on being served. So rather than engage in praying your loved one through a bad situation towards freedom, just issue the order for his immediate release and presentation before the court, and while he is in the presence of God, litigate his case and seek determination or final judgment. Why wait or travail for an extended period when such a remedy is available?

Following is an example of how to issue a habeas corpus order in prayer:

> You are the God who fights for me, who stands with me to deliver me, and who promises to protect the fruits from my womb and me from all harm and danger. I come boldly into Your inner courts and throw myself at Your feet, asking for Your mercy and grace to be extended towards [name the person], who has found himself swallowed up by the fiery pit of hell, with darkness slowly squeezing his life out of him. He is in the grip of [drugs, perversion, banditry, etc.], and my arm of love is unable to reach, release, or rescue him from the snares of the enemy. I have been walled off from him by [name friends, illegal activities, prison authorities, cult], and they seek after his life to destroy him. I ask for a habeas corpus order to be issued for him to be brought bodily into the heavenly court and in your presence, which is the only way for him to be saved. In the name of Your precious Son, Jesus Christ, I direct and order [name of the one holding the person or institution] that my [name person held] be presented bodily

before this heavenly court and there remain
until this matter concerning him is tried and
he is set free from the bondage of sin that
binds him. This order is signed and sealed
by Jesus Christ, in whose name is life and
freedom. Amen.

DECREES

Many people are familiar with issuing decrees and
declarations over situations in their lives. I have dealt
above with declarations and what these orders mean,
so it is expected that when they are applied, it is with
that explanation in mind. I have also dealt above, in
a glancing way, with what is meant by the issuance
of a decree, but I want to delve a bit deeper into this
concept. A recent development in Christian circles
that is fast becoming widespread is the mindless and
indiscriminate use of the words 'decree' and 'declare' as
intercessory prayer tools. Usually both words, 'decree'
and 'declare', are strung together by Christians during
prayer as a balm for all situations that arise. But do you
know what a decree is, or its purpose, limitation, or
scope? Do you know when to apply a decree in your
life or in what situations this will arise? Blind prayer
applications of decrees or declarations may not achieve
the intended or desired result; these requests may not
remove the problems. It is not in every situation or for

every problem that a decree will lie. In fact, the words 'decree' and 'declare' in a divorce order are not lumped together, as Christians habitually do in prayer, but are applied separately, in accordance with their meanings.

A decree is an official order or judgment with the force of law behind it. In the earthly court, a divorce decree will be granted, for example, to sever relationship ties. A decree is authoritative and unbreakable. There are two main types: a decree nisi, which is interim in nature and lasts for a stated timeframe, and a decree absolute, which terminates the marriage. Further, unless a decree nisi is pronounced absolute, the marital bonds are intact, for it is only a decree absolute which permanently and actually ends the marriage. The grant of a decree nisi comes attached with conditions and provides a period during which the parties are to sort out all other remaining marital issues. The petitioner is then required to take a step or approach the court for this decree to be made final. This comes only after the expiration of the stipulated period, and only if arrangements for children are satisfactorily made. What is sought is called the decree absolute; this is final or permanent in nature. Critical to note is that if this application for the decree absolute is never made or granted, the parties remain in law married; the marriage is not legally dissolved. If a person remarries with only a decree nisi in hand, he has run afoul of the law and can be charged with and convicted for bigamy.

So when you pray loosely, issuing decrees over every problem in your life, are these interim or final decrees? Are these rulings or orders available for your problems? Do the problems remain and re-manifest after the expiration of a fixed period? Do you understand the context in which the term decree is being used? When you 'decree and declare' that a problem relationship with a friend or co-worker is placed under a termination order or is severed, is that an interim or final order? If you unwittingly or unknowingly make a spiritual interim decree, do you move, in prayer, to make this absolute, or do you issue interim decrees over problems requiring decrees absolute, injunctive relief, or a warrant of arrest? Remember: God is calling us in this time to pray targeted and clear-cut prayers, and to engage in spiritual warfare with a knowing and skill that would make our enemies run and never return. Remember what a declaration is, and keep in mind that merely combining the words 'decree' and 'declare' does not bring about an absolute order; the nisi order must be made absolute or final by a follow-up order. The effect of a decree is to sever or dissolve the relationship, and a declaration confirms and affirms the cut as final, rendering it unchallengeable, unchangeable, and incontestable.

In another sense of its use, a decree refers to an enactment, law, or edict. Its use here is in the sense of an ordinance being proclaimed by a king, a head of state, or those with parliamentary authority. This occurs in Jonah 3:5–7 (KJV) when a fast is decreed by the king, as well as in Jeremiah 34:8–9 (KJV) when King Zedekiah proclaims a law to set all Hebrew servants free. If this is the sense in which it is being used in prayer, then understand that a statutory law is distinct from case law or an order of the court, which is law operationalized. The law set down in a statute or enactment is different from an order, which may be based on a statute but also on other precedents or decisions in cases. If a statutory law is broken, you will need to approach the earthly court for an order of the court to enforce it; it is not enforced by another enactment. If an order of the court or judgment is disobeyed, there are internal enforcement procedures in place in the court system, or another order will be issued to get compliance or punishment for breaches of the court order. In yet another sense of its use is the concept of decreeing, or when it takes the form of a transitive verb. In this sense, it refers to commanding or enjoining by decree or to determine or order something judicially such as to decree a punishment, or to decree an amnesty. This use of decree must be informed by an understanding of the context in which it can be utilised.

Following is an example of how to issue a decree to cut or end problems in relationships:

Precious Jesus, I present my application for a decree absolute to be issued in this relationship. I have attached to my application everything necessary to support my case, and I know You are aware of all things concerning this matter, for You said in Your word that You are touched with my infirmities. This problem, [name problem], has been ongoing for a while, and I have depleted my resources, time, and energy in seeking a resolution, but to no avail. I have issued numerous provisional decrees, but the problem remains. I hold that this relationship has broken down irretrievably and so is beyond repair or incapable of being salvaged. I now issue a decree that this problem, [name], is dissolved with the blood of Jesus Christ, for it is He alone who can end, sever, cut, disentangle, separate, and terminate this problem. There is no sufficient cause to be shown regarding why I should continue to suffer the indignity of this problem or maintain relationship ties with it. I declare that everything supports a confirmation that this problem stands dissolved, and I ask that time be abridged and my decree be pronounced as absolute. In the name of Jesus Christ, the interim decree first uttered to break this bond is declared as, and is now made, final and absolute. Amen.

INTERIM AND FINAL ORDERS

INTERIM ORDER

An interim or provisional order is also available in the civil courts for any number of matters – for example, to produce evidence and give directions to move your matter forward. These orders operate in much the same way as the decree nisi and are usually stated to be for a fixed period to get compliance. Interim orders are sometimes necessary to bring temporary relief in protracted litigation or to allow you to know what the case being raised against you by the other side is. An example of an interim order is a directions order or discovery order, which is an order to expose your documentary evidence, give the other side an opportunity to look at it and take copies, and set out steps to progress the matter to trial and completion. By looking at the other side's evidence, you can help build your case or prepare to answer the other side's case. Many of you already issue directions in your prayers for such information. In Christian circles, such an order is called a spiritual exposure order, which calls on God to expose the plans of the enemy with a view to destroying the works of the devil.

Another interim order is an amendment order, which seeks the permission of the court to change pleadings (or the case put forward), whether by adding or removing information provided. As Christians, we may at times have cause to amend the case we have before God, as further information becomes available. Remember: if you are praying for God to expose things to you, then when information is revealed you may need to amend how you have presented the problem to him. Yet another interim order is called an unless order, which is a requirement placed on one or both sides to comply with the directions of the court within a stipulated timeframe. It warns that failure to do so will attract immediate sanction. An unless order can lead to a dismissal of your case or some other 'hard' order, such as barring any further step being taken in the matter or preventing the use of some piece of evidence. It is useful for getting parties to comply in time with the court's directions. All these are useful tools to know because they help you to pray more on target. Hence, if you are uncertain as to how to pray concerning a matter, you may want to issue an interim order – as, in fact, many Christians already do.[13] So when you pray for God to expose a situation or someone's activities or to reveal what is going on in your husbands' or children's lives, or to reveal what evil is being plotted or executed against you, what you are in effect seeking is an interim order. Some people may take no further step once the information is revealed, while others will proceed to take steps to implement a final order, impose injunctive relief, or simply destroy the plot that was unearthed.

FINAL ORDER

A final or absolute order makes permanent whatever interim order is in place or moves a step further to apply the ultimate remedy to bring resolution to the problem. It is exactly what it is stated to be – an order that brings an end to the problem. An example of a final order is a judgment order. This being said, it is important to bear in mind that a final order may be subject to an appeal and so by extension can be overturned or confirmed. Once confirmed, then that is it; proceedings have ended completely. If overturned or reversed, you have to go through the process of re-litigating your matter, as the Court of Appeal can remit a matter back to the lower court to deal with it, based on its guidance. Or the Court of Appeal can replace an order that was appealed with its own order, which will now stand as the final order in the matter. Yes, appeals are costly in time, resources, and emotions, but when one is victorious in an appeal, it is exhilarating, boosts confidence, and vindicates your rights. Some judgment orders are framed in a way to prohibit a right to appeal; what is being carried out here is the prevention of a person from challenging your order. In prayer, if you are seeking a judgment order or final order, it is advisable to deny the enemy a right to appeal and so seal the prayer permanently from the mounting of any challenge to it.

Following are examples as to how interim and final orders are applied in prayer:

INTERIM ORDER, IN PRAYER

Father, I lift Your name up where it belongs, high above the heavens, and I give You thanks that You are the beginning and the ending of all things on earth and in heaven. You are the start, the continuation, and the end of all things good in my life. You take care of all my needs. You protect and deliver me from the snares and traps set by my enemies. You forewarn me of and reveal all things set against me and move to seal me off from harm. You have promised that though I walk through valleys of problems or encounter dark paths and even death, You will be there. You will shepherd and guide me safely through impassable terrain. You will show me how to slip out of the hands of the wicked, and You will reveal their evil devices and shield me from all harm. Now I find myself walking in uncertainty over this situation, [name situation], but I know and confess that You are the omniscient God and all knowledge is held by You.

I now seek Your directions as to how to proceed with this matter; I request Your help in uncovering and exposing the plans of the enemy. I refuse to wear spiritual or physical blinders any more, with respect to this problem. I desire to be in the know and to have revealed to me every foul plan of the enemy. I seek an order to expose, to uncover, to unearth, to extricate, excavate, and exhume every buried plan or thing hatched under, on, or above the earth that was set for my demise. I understand that I wrestle against principalities and powers and high things, so I ask for my enemy's plans to be revealed and laid bare before me to give me an insight as to how to engage him in this battle. I ask for permission to not only take copies of the enemy's plans but to also be given the strategy to eliminate these threats. I want to go into battle with a knowing which I don't currently have, so I ask for increased perception. I want a spiritual order of exposure of all the evil machinations, plans, and plots of the enemy so that I can examine them, make prints of them, and come up with a counterattack through Your Holy Spirit. Show me his plans, reveal his next step, expose his heart, and then give me the wisdom to devise the right offensive attack so that when I launch the second stage of my attack, he will not be able to stand or resist it. This interim order which I seek is for a period of three days – no longer, precious

Saviour – just enough time to understand, digest, and treat this problem. During this time, I will enter into a period of fasting to get clear directions on how to proceed and greater insight to order my steps. I seal this interim order with the blood of Jesus Christ. Amen.

FINAL ORDER, IN PRAYER

It is written that whatever I bind on earth shall be bound in heaven and whatever I loose on earth shall be loosed in heaven, for I have the keys that give me authority over the rulers of darkness and the principalities of the air. In the name of the most powerful, most holy, and most righteous God, the Almighty who is a consuming fire and the only undefeated king in war, I move to issue and make absolute this order against you, [name problem]. You have been exposed for the crafty, cunning, deceptive, slimy, wicked demonic weasel that you are, and your wicked plans are revealed and found deficient. You may have presented initially as strong, but the evidence shows you as weak and laughable. You are not permitted to stand, to battle, to raise a voice, or to take any further step to continue to perpetuate this problem. With immediate effect, final judgment is signed against you so you are stopped from continuing with or taking new steps in this battle against me (or my family, friend, or colleague). You have no right to bring fresh application or present new evidence, for your attack is ill-founded, weak, and feeble. I lock off any access you may have for issuing fresh proceedings against me in this matter. You have lost this battle once and for all. You are denied the right to continue with or to relaunch this attack – or, for that matter, any such attack – against me or anyone concerning me. You are charged with the responsibility to make recompense to me in this matter and to put me back in the position I was in prior to your attack. You will now vomit up, sweat out, bleed out, repay, recompense, replace, and reinstate all that you have stolen from me, in the name of Jesus Christ. All the money, riches, wealth, and property that you have stored up for future or pending attacks will now be used to recompense me for your daring to launch this attack against me. I leave you financially depleted and in poverty's hellhole from now on. There is no right of appeal of this order that is opened to you, and I seal off any crevice or slit through which you might aspire to crawl to rescind, set aside, or reverse this order. You are not at liberty to appeal this

order, for it is sealed with the blood of Jesus
Christ and signed with His name. Amen.

SETTING-ASIDE AND STRIKING-OUT ORDERS

Orders to set aside judgments or strike out parts of or
the whole case are granted during the course of the trial
and can be interim or final based on how the matter
progresses. I seek to explain them because they may be
useful praying tools for the trained orders expert. For
instance, in prayer you can make a request to have set
aside the case mounted against you by your enemy, a
judgment or order entered against you, or any problem
or issue plaguing you. Such an order is temporary in
nature, and while it brings relief, it does not permanently
seal off the other side from coming again or launching
an appeal. A problem or judgment that is set aside can
be restarted, because by its very nature, it is impossible
to seal off a setting-aside order from appeal. It is not a
final order, so a right of appeal will lie against it. So how
many of us, as Christians, pray for attacks against us to
be set aside, without understanding that this means it is
open for the enemy to come again with a fresh attack?
Do you understand why God is calling on you to be
specific in prayer? Once it is framed as a setting-aside
order, an appeal can be filed to challenge this order. So
when you pray to set things aside, be mindful that the
attack can be resumed. To set aside an attack provides

temporary relief, not complete reprieve, unless some further step is taken. The Bible is clear that an unclean spirit dispatched from a man can return to that clean house, but this fresh attack comes seven times worse. 'When the unclean spirit is gone out of a man, he walketh through dry places, seeking rest, and findeth none. Then he saith, I will return into my house from whence I came out; and when he is come, he findeth it empty, swept, and garnished. Then goeth he, and taketh with himself seven other spirits more wicked than himself, and they enter in and dwell there: and the last state of that man is worse than the first. Even so shall it be also unto this wicked generation' (Matthew 12:43–45 KJV).

While you are unable to barricade a setting-aside order from appeal or cannot deny the enemy the right to come again, you can be proactive in how you treat this order. Further, it is not every setting-aside order that is appealed, so understand that it is just open to appeal. Christians already pray to set aside decisions made against them, so it is useful to know how to use this method of praying effectively. Bear in mind that praying against a decision made against you and asking for it to be set aside is proper and useful. In fact, without the setting-aside order, that decision (in law it is called 'procedural decision') has the effect of a final judgment, because it is left undisturbed by you – hence the grave importance of seeking and obtaining a setting-aside order. Once this is done, you can use your spiritual monitors to watch over this order to see if a fresh attack resumes and be ready to battle it out in the spiritual Court of Appeal. What obtains or occurs at the appellate level is discussed below so you can understand why I have no problem issuing the interim setting-aside order and why I wait for the enemy to dare to appeal it. I do not stand down from any opportunity to engage in heightened warfare or to put an advanced appellate whipping on my enemy. It is in the spiritual Appellate Court that your skills as an orders expert will be honed, sharpened, and increased.

With respect to a striking-out order, this too is generally interim in nature and subject to appeal. A striking-out application seeks to have removed parts or portions of the case mounted against you, for reason. By this it is meant that the applicant must show cause as to why he wants pieces of the case struck out. Application can also be made here for the entire case to be struck out, in which case the striking-out order, if granted, is a final order. On the other hand, if the interim striking-out order (according to which only parts of the case are struck out) is not appealed, then it stands as final. Final here does not end the matter; it means you can proceed now to trial on the remaining parts of the case. Whether this refers to parts of the case that are struck off or the entire matter, it cannot be sealed off from appeal. So be careful, when you pray, to make orders that could be sealed off from appeal, and know the value of those that cannot be made immune from an appeal. Both types of orders are useful in their own context, and are not to be disregarded as praying tools. The importance of a striking-out order is that (by removing pieces or parts of the evidence) it weakens the enemy's case. A skilled orders expert will use this tool to weaken the enemy, recharge, and then launch a full-scale missile attack to destroy him. So do not avoid its use; learn its value and how to use it strategically in spiritual warfare. Become spiritual orders strategists, skilled tacticians, master planners, specialist negotiators, and dangerous plotters of the spiritual demise of your enemy. The devil may be roaming about, seeking whom to destroy, but he is not expecting spiritual warfare strategists, skilled and waiting to snipe his head off. The Bible tells us: 'Be sober, be vigilant; because your adversary the devil, as a roaring lion, walketh about, seeking whom he may devour' (1 Peter 5:8 KJV). We are not told to stand down or run away; if anything, the Bible is clear that we are to train in becoming orders experts by setting out many strategies for spiritual engagements. (See Ephesians 6:11–18 KJV.)

PAYMENT OUT AND PAYMENT IN ORDERS

Orders to pay monies in or out of court are types of interim orders. Christians frequently seek a payment out from God's storehouse and so are versed in these requests. Monies are deposited into court pursuant to a statutory rule, order, or settlement offer, and parties then seek orders for payment out. Christians too make these applications for financial rewards, many of which are grounded in or guided by divine principles, such as giving (see Luke 6:38 KJV), tithing (see Malachi 3:10 and 2 Chronicles 31:12 KJV), and doing the work of His kingdom (see Matthew 6:31–34). You need to pray with the confidence, proper mindset, and understanding that your order will be granted because of His Word. The Bible is clear that He wishes above all things that you might prosper and be in good health. (See 3 John 1:2 KJV.)

JUDGMENT ORDER

A judgment order is one that most people seek and are familiar with, so I could not fail to address it in this book. 'A judgment order' is the term used in the civil court and is usually the place where this type of order is obtained. A judgment order is a final order. It is different from a conviction or sentencing (which relate to criminal proceedings), although these are all decisions of the court that bring matters to an end. Most people are quite familiar with a conviction or sentence and so can pray with the understanding of their impact on lives, so I will not deal with those here. A judgment order is a slightly more complicated construct, as it covers a number of situations. Subsumed under this concept of a judgment will be orders for judgments in default of taking or complying with a required step in the proceedings or judgment on admission, so you need to be clear what you are praying for – especially as the first one can be interim in nature, as it is open to being set aside. Remember: I have explained above that orders are specific, and to use them in a generalised way may affect the significance of their impact. Do not just ask for judgment in your favour when you pray; say what you want judgment for, the type of judgment and the terms of the judgment you want against your enemy. Be specific in prayer, and be careful to set out the exact judgment sought. Remember: any order can be subject to appeal, so ensure that your judgment order is not appealed. These are the most frequently appealed orders, and in like manner, if you are not specific, you may set yourself up for an appeal.

Following is an example of issuing a judgment order in prayer:

> Father, I place this issue of [name issue] at the feet of Your heavenly court, for it is only there that it can be resolved. I lay bare before You all the evidence, accepting that there is nothing that remains undiscovered or hidden from You. The evidence points to liability being found in my enemy's actions and a tort (wrong) having been done to me. He has defaulted in presenting a wholesome and

strong case and now stands responsible to compensate me for the wrong done to me in this cause. I ask for judgment to be entered in my favour for a return to me of [state what judgment you want (e.g., promotion, fertility, marriage, health, etc.)] and that I be reinstated to the place I was in prior to his attack. I seek only a final judgment as my enemy is liable (or responsible) in this matter for having trespassed upon, removed, or destroyed what is lawfully mine and must restore unto me my rightful inheritance. My property is mine, my home is mine, my children are mine, the issues of my womb are mine, my health is mine, and my promotion is mine and shall remain mine in perpetuity. You – wicked, scheming foe – will not flee with or deprive me of my possessions.

I order you to return everything that you have appropriated wrongfully as yours right back to me. You are held responsible for the wrong you have committed against me and are found liable. You are ordered to pay compensation to me by returning threefold what was stolen. You are also ordered to pay me costs for the inconvenience I have suffered in this matter and the time and energy expended or wasted in defending your attack. You will recompense me for everything you have put me through. This order is blood sealed and signed with the hand of Jesus Christ. You are denied the liberty or right to appeal this judgment. It stands unimpeachable and immune from being set aside, reversed, or revoked. There is no right of challenge or appeal against this judgment order, and your culpability is confirmed. I have ordered no stay on this order, so compensation attaches now, in the name of Jesus Christ. Amen.

DAMAGES ORDER

Another name for a damages order is 'compensatory order'. Such an order is for monetary compensation to be awarded to you for a wrong done. This may be a useful prayer to utter and to mandate that you be granted compensation for what you have been put through. Compensation here speaks strictly of monetary compensation. This payment is usually awarded in two main components. For example, you may ask for general compensation for your pain and suffering and other losses sustained, which is a sum that is not identified; or for special damages, which allows you to specify the figure you think will satisfy you. You can also ask for compensation for any future losses that you anticipate will arise from this battle. In fact, when you are asking to get compensation following an attack from the enemy, release the stored-up wealth he holds for you: '…the wealth of the sinner is laid up for the just' (Proverbs 13:22 KJV). If you are in warfare and get injured, you are entitled to get compensation.

GAG ORDER

This order is used to prevent a particular type of undesirable or unsavoury behaviour. A gag order, or suppression order, is a directive from a judge forbidding the public disclosure of information on a particular matter. It is often used to prevent newspapers or other media from printing or commenting on sensitive information that comes out in open court during proceedings. And in the spiritual world, it can be used similarly to suppress or clamp down on the spread of information.

As Christians, we go through painful and sensitive periods in life during which our suffering becomes fodder for others to feed on, converse about, share via social media, and even to rejoice and salivate over. This can be particularly painful when it is our own Christian brothers and sisters engaged in this practice, rather than praying about the situation. How many of us share the gossip in church without giving a second thought to our action being insensitive, unwise, and condemned? (See Ephesians 4:29–31 KJV and James 1:26; 4:11 KJV.) How often are gossipers in the church rebuked for being 'not only idle, but tattlers also and busybodies, speaking things which they ought not' (1 Timothy 5:13 KJV), yet this practice is not stemmed?

The social media trend of feasting on, sharing, and sensationalising the misfortunes of others is now the latest Christian fab. We are fast becoming so desensitised that the impact of our actions is not even appreciated. I call it the 'social media *corbeaux* mentality'.[14] In Trinidad, where I am from, these corbeaux are vultures that circle around and feast on the entrails of carcasses. So when you engage in sharing on social media the pictures of 'Christian' or churchgoing adulterers, instead of praying, it is displaying the corbeaux mentality. When you indiscriminately share videos on social media of the falls of prophets and pastors as well as of abuse being meted out to a Christian brother or sister in his or her marriage, instead of praying, it is displaying the corbeaux mentality. It is against such untoward information sharing that a spiritual gag order will lie and be most applicable. A spiritual gag order operates to stop the flow of unholy, unrighteous, and judgmental conversations, as it did when God rebuked Aaron and Miriam for speaking ill of Moses and then gagged her with leprosy and expulsion for a period. (See Numbers 12:1–15 KJV.)

Committal Order

A committal order is one directing that a person be placed in prison upon a breach of a court order or as the result of contempt of court. It usually forms part of an injunctive order and specifies that if the injunction is breached, the person will be committed to prison. However, it can be sought for any other breaches of court orders. So it is wise, when you are issuing injunctive orders in prayer, to insert at the end a committal order, to read as follows: 'You are hereby commanded to and compelled to abide by, observe, and obey this order. If you disobey this order, you will be in contempt of this heavenly court and liable to seizure of assets, fines, penalties, or committal, in Jesus' name. Amen.'

Appeal Order

On appeal, an order may be reversed, set aside, upheld (affirmed and confirmed), or overturned. There are two aspects to consider here: first, you can appeal decisions entered against you; and secondly, the orders you make in spiritual warfare can be appealed, revoked, or reversed, so you are required to seal off your orders from being overturned. Not every decision is appealed, so you are to ensure that the orders you issue in prayer do not attract a notice of appeal. And be mindful that if there is any negative order issued against you, you understand that you retain a right of appeal and move to overturn it.

An appeal prayer asks for the heavenly Appellate Court to reconsider the decision, to give it a second look, and to have more than one person adjudicate on it, with a view to reversing or overturning the decision made against you (or of affirming or confirming an order you have made). An appeal order is final once it comes from the final Appellate Court – that is, once there is no other court to which it can be sent. So be careful, in prayer, to seal your appeals off with the stamp of the heavenly Court of Appeal. In spiritual warfare, battling against principalities and spiritual wickedness in high places can be most rewarding when done in the Appellate Court. It is a place made for heightened battle, where the war engaged in serves to annihilate, defeat, and crush the attack launched against you but also sets the precedent to be followed by the other courts. The heavenly Appellate Court is the place for thrashing and overwhelming the enemy with a different level of intensity that sends a resounding message not to mess with you. A battle won there leaves the devil spent, charred, and burnt out, and the reversed decision must be adhered to by all. An appeal order sets the precedent; in other words, it is what must be followed.

If the decision (attack) is against you, exercise your right to appeal by taking it straight to the spiritual Court of Appeal. A spiritual Court of Appeal is where many spiritual battles play out. Christians are to reject and not to tolerate decisions made against them unjustly, such as one failing to get a promotion one has worked hard for – especially when the person getting the promotion is lazy or incompetent but knows how to outmanoeuvre you by marketing himself as more deserving. Take it to the spiritual Court of Appeal and have that decision reversed or overturned, and demand a reconsideration of the matter.

There are several instances in the Bible of appeals being made for a reconsideration of decisions, and orders being issued by the spiritual Appellate Court, overturning decisions that had been made. For example, Hezekiah's life, which was under a death sentence, was extended by fifteen years, upsetting or overthrowing the order that he would die and not live. (See Isaiah 38:1–5 KJV.) If you are ill and have been given an expiry date by doctors, take it to the spiritual Court of Appeal and have that order overthrown and replaced with an order for the extension of your lifespan. Yes, an extension-of-time order is a type of order available in a civil court and is frequently applied for and granted. Another ripe example for the spiritual Court of Appeal is the case where a decision is made in the pit of hell to deny you from the joy of experiencing motherhood. Take it to the spiritual Court of Appeal. The righteous seed is entitled to come forth, to prosper, and to enjoy the promises of God concerning him. (See Genesis 22:15–18 KJV and

Psalm 89:4 KJV.) When you are dismissed from your job unjustly or without cause, head straight to the spiritual Court of Appeal with that decision. When your boss accuses you of something unjustly or treats you unfairly by demoting you, go upstairs to the Appellate Court. There are some Christians who are struggling on their jobs with oppressive supervisors who continually make decisions to keep them in a state of stress and fear. Instead of transferring out, taking early retirement, remaining silent, praying soft prayers, or operating in denial, appeal the decisions and get reversal orders. When a decision is taken to steal your wife or husband and leave your children motherless or fatherless, march upstairs to the spiritual Court of Appeal. When you are refused a bank loan for no just reason, seek a reversal order. Appeals will be available when the promises of God for your life are under attack and blocked from manifesting through unjust and ungodly decisions. An appeal can reverse those wrong decisions. Let your mantra be 'Take it to the spiritual Court of Appeal (repeat); we are reversing that order, overturning it, and setting it aside, for we are not taking that.'

Here is how to appeal an order or a ruling against you:

You are a great God; everything about You is great. You are an awesome God, and I am awestruck when I think of You. You are a Mighty God, and everything appears frail in your presence. So it is in Your just nature, God, that I seek reprieve, shelter, and protection. When the waters rise up against me and seek to drown me, I remember the Almighty, the Great I am that I am, and the Just and Holy One; and I recall that in You is hidden my reward. Justice is You and You are Justice; You are inseparable from it, and it is an intrinsic part of who You are. You sit at the helm of the heavenly Appellate Court, rendering just and holy decrees, pronouncements, declarations, and orders. Your rulings are immune from appeal, and there is only fairness and justice handed down by You. You are the Alpha and the Omega, the beginning and the end in terms of justice; what You pronounce must stand as final. You cannot dispense injustice or stand unmoved by unjust rulings. Your inner being is fair, Your rulings are beyond reproach and just, and no wrong judgment can stand in Your presence.

Most just God, I approach as one wronged, as one blocked from Your promise that I would be promoted [or 'bring forth righteous seeds', or name the promise] but who refuses to be squeezed out or accept anything except Your word concerning my life. Yes, a grave error was done to me by this order under which I stand accused or denied access to what You have already established is mine. Erroneous findings have been made against me, precious Lord. I have been found undeserving [or 'guilty'] without a proper hearing. My enemies have conspired in secret to pull me down and destroy me. So I turn to You, most holy and just God, to seek justice by filing with You a notice containing my request to overturn (or revoke or reverse) this decision under which I stand denied [or 'rejected', 'condemned', or 'liable']. I lay my case at the feet of this heavenly Court of Appeal, present the unjust treatment meted out to me, and plead my innocence in this matter. I did not commit the wrong for which I now stand condemned, and I do not deserve to be denied or barred from [name specific complaint (e.g., promotion, bringing forth children)], so I seek an order overturning this decision. I present my evidence and ask that You take a fresh look and do justice by me. I thank You, Lord, for restoring all that was taken from me, and for reversing, overturning, erasing, and blotting out the writings against me from this lower court. I thank You for now affirming and confirming my right to bear children ['promotion', 'health', 'family life', etc.] and repeat Your order thus:

In the name of Jesus Christ, this order or decision of the court below against [insert name] life is reversed, overturned, revoked, and set aside. The appeal against this order of the lower court is hereby allowed, and in its place a different order is issued in the following terms: [State the terms of the new order]. [Insert your name] is delivered from the bondage under which ['he' or 'she'] was placed and is set free to walk in the purpose for which ['he' or 'she'] was created, without interference from ['his' or 'her'] enemies. ['He' or 'She'] is found not liable in this matter, and all previous orders issued against ['him' or 'her'] are removed and reversed now, in the precious name of Jesus Christ. Amen.

Here is how to seal off an order issued by you from an appeal:

[After issuing your order, say the following.]

Any appeal of this order is denied outright and upfront. Any right or liberty to appeal that you, (problem, enemy, or opposing party), claim is hereby removed from you, and you will remain bound by my order as if it were issued by a final Appellate Court. You will not be able to file any notice of appeal or seek a hearing from or approach justices of appeal who sit in a higher court to overturn this order. This order is declared as a final order and is sealed with the stamp of Jesus Christ and signed with His blood. It cannot be overturned, revoked, reversed, set aside, or overthrown. It stands as ordered, in the name of Jesus Christ. Amen.

CHAPTER 7

WHY BE AN ORDERS EXPERT?

An orders expert is one who is equipped with the proper understanding of how and when spiritual orders are to be issued and why a particular order is more relevant to resolving a specific problem. An orders expert is also one possessing a heightened sense of discernment and perception, which are relevant for effective functioning in spiritual warfare in this end-time period. God who is order is desirous of His people becoming spiritually sharpened to all that is unfolding globally and to their becoming strategists and skilled tacticians in spiritual warfare. The call to become an orders expert is a request of God to His people to see Him as order and then image Him. It is a call to become highly trained specialists in the art of battling using spiritual orders. It challenges the believer to ascend to the proper positioning for spiritual warfare and unleash a full-scale war against the devil (who is the principality of disorder) and his minions, with a view to annihilating them completely. The purposes for becoming an orders expert are multi-fold, and a few are examined going forward.

TO SHARPEN BELIEVERS' STRATEGIC WARFARE SKILLS

This is one of the imperatives of becoming an orders expert, as we are involved in spiritual warfare, where non-experts are likely to be trampled under the feet of the skilled forces of the enemy. Believers need to be involved in strategic spiritual warfare or pray tactically, because the devil and his underlings are trained in strategic spiritual warfare. This is not to say that God will not fight for you if you are unskilled, or send His spiritual battle forces to defend you, but it increases the value and contribution of the believer if he or she becomes skilled in spiritual warfare. Why be a wounded troop if you can be in the position of doing the wounding? Why allow the devil and his cohorts to have you on the run, when God says you are to put the devil and his associates to flight? What then is strategic spiritual warfare or a warfare strategist? Simply put, a spiritual warfare strategist is a planner, a tactician, and a plotter; he or she is a person who enters warfare prayer or spiritual battles with an advanced perspective on likely attacks and with ready solutions. Strategic warfare is more than just being thoughtful or considered when engaging the principalities and dark spirits of wickedness that inhabit the spiritual realm. It involves having the foresight and perception to anticipate the attacks of the demonic troops and to intercept them in the spiritual realm before they manifest on the earth. It is about developing and honing creative warfare skills in prayer by being premeditated, tactical, and intentional in launching attacks against the devil and warding off demonic assaults. It is about outmanoeuvring the devil and his troops with the use of an advanced line of attack and stratagems.

The call to strategic spiritual warfare or to become a prayer expert is a heavenly demand upon believers to be offensive and defensive in prayer. It is a call to become skilled at planning attacks and being defensive in spiritual battles, and to be spiritual warfare specialists and planners and so take the enemy by surprise and have him constantly on the run. It is not about praying the same way or using the same words all the time, or even allowing the devil to anticipate and time your prayer engagements. The devil should not be able to anticipate your prayer manoeuvers or counterattack prayer missiles launched against his forces. It is not about engagement without understanding or mimicking of nice-sounding words and phrases and feeling that by doing the same you will somehow impact the kingdom of darkness. You cannot be praying the same way for years, getting the same answers or non-answers, and continuing to do it without change and expecting to get a different response.

Strategic prayer is about understanding your approach, standing, and positioning, knowing the orders you have the authority to issue in prayer, and knowing how to do so. It is not about blindly and erroneously using 'prayer words' or tricking yourself into believing that the more times you utter them, the more likely they will be to eventually work. In the military circles, there are certain high-end units whose skills, stratagems, and the authority with which they operate have earned them respect and a presence that brokers no resistance when they engage in warfare. They conduct covert operations and can get in and out of enemy territory and do lethal damage to their opponents' property and men without the enemy even being aware of what happened until long after the operation has ended. Strategic prayer is much like that; it is a method of launching unanticipated attacks against the enemy, whipping and stripping him of any advantage he has, and leaving him confused about what has happened. Strategic prayer involves operating like those high-end, highly skilled military units or specialist forces whose training and operations are clandestine and targeted to maximise results. Remember: when Satan instigated the downfall of man and succeeded in getting Adam to sin, he was unaware that the God who is order was 'sequencing the events' and had waiting in the wings His master strategy to bring glory to His name – His Son, Jesus Christ. Strategic prayer is about inhabiting that place, in prayer, where your voice, as a man, becomes the voice of God. It is about becoming highly skilled strategists and prayer specialists who will target and destroy the forces of darkness, without them even being aware of what is happening. It is about becoming orders experts.

TO IMAGE GOD

An orders expert's mandate is to image order, which effectively is to be a copy or print of God who is order. It is understood that we are to be order and to operate with the power and authority He wields in spiritual warfare and from that advantageous positioning. This is done by inhabiting His presence and adopting His spirit and power in battling principalities and powers of darkness. When the image of God becomes the attire we present, it is like wearing His presence so that our faces shine (much like Moses' did), in order that darkness will not be able to engage us in battle but will flee from us. Remember that demons tremble in the presence of Jesus and unclean spirits recognise Him and beg Him not to torment them. (See Mark 5:1–17 KJV and James 2:19 NIV.) That is the same authority we will walk in and exercise over the forces of darkness and even greater authority. When we ascend to this level in spiritual warfare, we not only dispel darkness but also achieve the purposes for which we were created.

TO WALK IN OBEDIENCE

Obedience is a mandatory requirement for being an orders expert, for it is the mirror image of order. When we walk in obedience to the will of God and become orders experts, we are equipping ourselves with the winning strategy for engagement in spiritual warfare in these final days. You would have learnt above how central obedience is to restoring order. It took Christ's obedience by submitting to the death of the cross to wash away the disobedience of Adam, which had created the wedge between God and man. In these final days, we are called to be obedient – to choose order and submit to becoming orders experts so that our engagement in the end-time battle will be targeted and precise.

TO OPERATE IN INCREASED PERCEPTION AND DISCERNMENT

At this particular time in Christian history, having increased perception and discernment must be the ultimate goal of every believer. These are the spiritual tools that are necessary as the last resort for decimating the devil in strategic warfare. Without heightened perception and increased discernment, believers will be taken by surprise in spiritual battles rather than doing what they have been called to do – confuse and scatter the forces of evil by operating ahead of them. For too long, Christians have been reacting to demonic attacks rather than being spiritually proactive and launching attacks against the devil to confuse and undermine his every plan. How many of us spend countless hours praying against what the devil has done to our lives? Well, that needs to stop. Instead of praying against the work of the devil, spend time seeking God for enhanced perception to see the devil's attacks before they are launched or even hatched in the pit of hell. Ask for discernment so your eyes and ears will behold the activities of those plotting your demise in the pit of darkness, and ask for the creative strategies to attack, even as the plots are being hatched. Heightened perception will allow believers to know what the enemy is planning and to plan ahead of him, plot his downfall, launch the attack against him, and get out of his space before he perceives what has hit him. Becoming an orders expert will allow you to think ahead and use the skills you are honing to outwit the devil.

TO FULFIL GOD'S END-TIME AGENDA ON EARTH

God's final agenda on earth is to completely decimate disorder and restore order. We are becoming orders experts to provide God with a highly trained spiritual force that is capable of wiping the devil from the earth. The devil is disorder. The truth of this statement lies in the nature of the enemy, whose sole aim is to contest the order that God represents. Other spirits come along with the head spirit of disorder, so becoming an orders expert is a means of tooling yourself to be a more effective and targeted warrior. As an orders expert, you will become sensitised to the plurality of weapons at your disposal to fight against disorder and its demonic spirits – particularly the spirits of self and disobedience.

For months prior to God's direct order to me to write this book, He was ministering to me about the spirit of self and exposing its many manifestations and treachery. This spirit of self is one of the most dangerous and lethal spirits in the arsenal of disorder. It is duplicitous, deceptive, manipulative, selfish, proud, self-centred, and self-promoting, and it has zero time or interest for anything but its own agenda and the feeding of its own flesh. It is the same spirit epitomised by Lucifer, which drove him to rebel and be thrown out of heaven. It is the same spirit that is operating in the modern world and manifesting in the new waves of populism and nationalism that are sweeping across the political globe. The spirit of self wants it all for itself; it does not care about others and is singly the most selfish, traitorous, and double-crossing of spirits that will stop at nothing to promote itself. The spirit of self appears subtle, innocuous, and non-suspect, and it argues for the promotion of the good of self. Self is quintuplicated with disorder, disobedience, chaos, and confusion. These spirits operate together, along with a host of others, so it is critical for the church to be discerning in this time as to how these end-time spirits operate. When we become orders experts, we allow ourselves to become more discerning and perceptive and thus better equipped to decimate disorder.

Becoming an orders expert is a critical end-time requirement for every believer to be trained in, for it will facilitate spiritual growth and help believers build a solid wall of defence against the wiles of the enemy, from behind which they can launch attacks. Becoming orders experts will help usher in God's end-time agenda on this chaotic earth by preparing His army for the return of order.

Orders Expert

I'm plotting and planning, purposing your demise
In training to war, on bended knees I'm bombarding
your plans
Dismissing, restraining, gagging your words, and
foiling your plots
For I'm a tactician sure, a prayer strategist pure, taking
it no more
Shelving self and unsheathing God, wounding Satan
with my sword
Ordering his destruction, committing, binding,
spiritually kicking him sore
Executing His plan, to be His image in this land
For I'm an expert in orders, fighting this war
I've got grounding, standing, and positioning galore
One of His chosen generation of royal blood
Equipped with spiritual weapons, well skilled and
victorious in battle
For I'm an orders expert, and I AM, Divine Order,
is God!

Martha Lynette Alexander
1 May 2017

ENDNOTES

1 Bligh: a free pass or an excuse for not doing something.

2 W. E. Vine, Merrill F. Unger, and William White Jr., *Vine's Complete Expository Dictionary of Old and New Testament Words*, (Nashville, Tennessee: Thomas Nelson) 450.

3 Strong's Hebrew Concordance www.biblehub.com/Hebrew/6186.htm (accessed on 12.04.17)

4 In Genesis 1:1–3, the godhead in action is also presented; there is God, the Creator; the Holy Spirit, the Mover; and Jesus Christ, the Light of the world. In these three representations, God is order.

5 See chapter 6, 'Types of Orders 2', for more on declaratory orders.

6 The godhead is presented as order in Genesis 1:1–3 and John 1:1.

7 *King James Version Life in the Spirit Study Bible* (Grand Rapids, Michigan: Zondervan, 2003).

8 Vine, 450.

9 www.biblehub.com/HELPSWord-studies/(Helps Ministries, Inc., 2011), <TheDiscoveryBible.com>.

10 The word 'interest' is used here in its legal sense of having some right to be heard.

11 Warrants in criminal matters include bench warrants (usually issued in traffic matters for a failure to appear),

search warrants, and arrest warrants. In civil matters, a fugae warrant can be issued to apprehend an absconding debtor.

12 Other injunctive orders include the Anton Piller order, which is a search warrant that gives access to a defendant's premises to search and seize evidence without prior notice to him. This aims to prevent a defendant from disposing of or destroying important evidence that a claimant may need to prove his case. Additionally, a Mareva injunction is an order that freezes a debtor's assets to prevent them from being taken abroad. These are both interim orders.

13 Other types of interim orders are orders for substitution, variation, wasted costs, extension of time (e.g., for your life span to be expanded), winding up orders, maintenance, or expert evidence, just to list a few.

14 This refers to a black vulture (*Ceoragyps alratus*), also called 'cordeau', from the French word 'Le Corbeau', for 'raven'.

ABOUT THE AUTHORS

Martha Lynette Alexander is an author, attorney at law, teacher, and master of the High Court of Trinidad and Tobago but believes that it is her relationship with Jesus Christ that is, by far, her most significant accomplishment. She was born in Trinidad and Tobago and has used the pen to highlight troubling societal issues and to teach persons of all ages to write properly. In 2008, she published *Language Alternative: For Teaching Writing Skills* in the United Kingdom. She is currently an adjunct lecturer at the Law School in Trinidad and Tobago, where she teaches on crafting and issuing legal orders, among other things, so when the call came by God for her to present Him as order, she was able to provide a unique and interesting perspective on spiritual orders. She also served as a Bible school lecturer and youth ministry leader in the past, and at present she mentors young men and women in crisis. Martha tells anyone who is willing to listen that when she gave her life to Jesus Christ at the age of nineteen, it was His to use to bring glory to His name. She believes that true service to God comes from a position of humility and selflessness – important aspects of imaging God – so she strives daily to demonstrate Christ through mimicking the way He walked humbly, honestly, and obediently on earth.

Natasha Cumberbatch Ryan has a passion for teaching, which she has been doing since the age of eighteen. While she has always embraced her gift for teaching and pursued it zealously, she knew that her anointing transcended the classroom. It has spilled over into all aspects of her life – particularly her desire to impact the body of Christ. She has served as a youth teacher and prayer ministry leader, but more so as a spiritual mentor to several of her personal friends and students. She holds the scripture 2 Peter 1:3 ESV close to her heart; she desires to be more and more like Christ, to be a true disciple of His, to be led on a path where she can impact the lives of all those who are called by His name and to admonish them that their example in the heavenly realm has equipped them with every good and righteous gift to carry out His will on the earth.

Printed in the United States
By Bookmasters